# Introduction

As our Father does his works in our lives, he graciously intersects our path with the many he has prepared in advance to help us. While "*Life, Love and Leading*" has been a work in process for nearly 20 years, its preparation has spanned my lifetime and required the faithful input of hundreds.

What follows is the *Love* section. "*Love*" expands upon the prayers Jesus taught us, that we better understand their depth and impact as prayers for the whole world. Further, regarding ourselves, it facilitates *Life* transformation through our conversations with Adonai (our triune God) and each other as he leads us through each day.

*There is a cosmic battle going on between God and his Enemies for the lives of every person and nation on earth. Will you pass down the love of God to your children, that they then pass it down to their childrens' children? Will you share the love of God as he places someone in your path today? As we learn to live with hearts after the Father and in the attitudes of the Beatitudes (Jesus' attitudes), this posture and humility will prepare us for fruit of the Spirit language and actions in each and every interaction.*
*That none should perish.*

The wisdom that follows does not so much come from me, but from a lifetime of collaborating with God and the many wise counselors he has put in my path. Proverbs 11:14 tells us that where there is no guidance the people fall, but in an abundance of counselors there is victory. May it be so for you as you invite Adonai in to grow you through the teaching and training of Jesus, reflection upon the prayers he taught us, and the leading of the Holy Spirit - as the Father does his works in us.

*As God's righteousness flows through us, Jesus said that our prayers will avail much! So, pray the prayers he taught us, as he taught us, for the whole world! Be in conversational worship all day long! That our children know him, our families be strong, and the division & disintegration of our nations be reversed.*

# Love

## "Lord, teach us how to pray."

## Contemplations on the Prayers Jesus Taught Us

**From the book**

# Life, Love & Leading

## Love



All scripture is English Standard Version (ESV) unless otherwise indicated.

# Love

## *Chapter One*

### Talmidim *Becoming* More And More Like Jesus

In Jesus' day, the clear responsibility of the rabbi was to teach them "how to fulfill the Torah". That is to say, "how to live a life pleasing to God". The *Life* section describes it in great detail. In fact, our entire Bible emphasizes it. Our church leaders carry this responsibility today, as do any who call themselves one of his disciples.

But what does it mean to be his disciple? It is probably different than you think because we do not have any word for it in our English language. The Hebrew word translated for us to English is *talmid*. The plural is *talmidim*. Talmidim are what we in the USA erroneously call "disciples, students and apprentices":

*Unlike the words disciple or student or apprentice that suggest a learning and doing process, the word talmid is a Hebrew term that describes a becoming process. Talmidim desire to become just like their rabbi. It is more than the practical application of the knowledge gained. It is more than taking actions based upon our understanding of his teachings. It was not just to know what the rabbi knew, but to be what the rabbi was.*

*A talmid of Rabbi Jesus will have a heart after the Father, be growing to reflect the very character of Jesus and be gaining the mind and attitudes of Christ. Jesus came to live it out as an example for us, his heart after the Father's, doing all his will. He taught and showed us how to live a life pleasing to God.*

Spending every minute of every day with their rabbi, talmidim would watch and see and hear and learn *how* he helped people understand and fulfill the Torah. Both by his words and by his actions, that they would *become* just like him.

*It was not just to know what the rabbi knew, but to be what the rabbi was.*

Unfortunately, much of what most present-day pastor/teachers do is provide head knowledge for our choosing in a particular *life application*. These take the individualistic *Hellenistic* approach rather than the *talmidic* approach, and it may be the biggest reason that the church in the USA has been in decline for so very many decades.

****************

When Jesus said go and make talmidim of all nations, he did not say go and teach people the bible so that they could practically apply the information to their lives, he said to go help people *become* just like him! Between the *what to know* and the *how to live*, he spent more time on the *how – how to live a life pleasing to God.*

Two thousand years later, we have lost the context of this and many other portions of scripture. Because we are not from that era, we have also lost the images his Hebrew and Aramaic words would immediately evoke culturally in their listeners.

If *we* will endeavor to *become* just like Jesus, the making of talmidim will require *individual* conversational time with others in ongoing *life-on-life* discussion. Not forsaking the fellowship, a talmid will also be associated with some sort of *group* of talmidim - continually discussing *how to live the life of a talmid*. Not only that, but *how to help others understand what it means* to live a life pleasing to God.

As described in great detail in *Life*, becoming like Jesus:

- *I only say and do what the Father gives me to say and do.*
- *I see what the Father is doing and behave likewise.*
- *I do nothing of my own accord.*
- *I do as the Father commands, that the world may know I love the Father.*
- *Unless I come as a child, I will never enter the Kingdom of heaven.*
- *My sheep know my voice and they follow.*
- *...for apart from Him I can do nothing.*
- *Blessed am I when I live, move and breathe in His attitudes.*

*Deuteronomy 18:18*

*I will raise up for them a prophet like you (Moses) from among their fellow Israelites, and I will put my words into his mouth. He will tell them everything I command him.*

*John 12:49-50*

*49 For I have not spoken on my own authority, but the Father who sent me has himself given me a commandment—what to say and what to speak. 50 And I know that his commandment is eternal life. What I say, therefore, I say as the Father has told me."*

*John 14:10*

*Do you not believe that I am in the Father and the Father is in me? The words that I say to you I do not speak on my own authority, but the Father who dwells in me does his works.*

*John 5:19*

*So Jesus said to them, "Truly, truly, I say to you, the Son can do nothing of his own accord, but only what he sees the Father doing. For whatever the Father does, that the Son does likewise.*

*John 14:30-31*

*30 I will no longer talk much with you, for the ruler of this world is coming. He has no claim on me, 31 but I do as the Father has commanded me, so that the world may know that I love the Father.*

*Matthew 18:1-4*

*1 At that time the disciples came to Jesus, saying, "Who is the greatest in the kingdom of heaven?" 2 And calling to him a child, he put him in the midst of them 3 and said, "Truly, I say to you, unless you turn and become like children, you will never enter the kingdom of heaven. 4 Whoever humbles himself like this child is the greatest in the kingdom of heaven.*

*John 10:27*

*My sheep hear my voice, and I know them, and they follow me.*

*John 15:5*

*I am the vine; you are the branches. Whoever abides in me and I in him, he it is that bears much fruit, for apart from me you can do nothing.*

What did he say at the Last Supper, on the night he was betrayed? "Do this in remembrance of me."

Most of my life my remembrance during Communion has been of his suffering and death on my behalf. The whipping, the beatings, the crown of thorns, the nails, the mocking, the anguish, hanging there, rejected, in excruciating pain… and finally, death. His saving sacrifice.

But, I think, this is not what he wants *most* to be remembered for. Time after time throughout his life he pointed people to our Father in heaven. It doesn't make sense to me that what he wants to do now is point us to himself rather than our Father. No, it seems more likely that what he wants us to remember about him is that he *only said and did what our Father gave him to say and do.* Throughout his entire life. All the way to the end of it:

He trained the 12, setting into motion the making of talmidim with the 70, the 500 and eventually people in every nation on earth.
He went to Jerusalem, knowing what would happen there.
He told Judas to get on with it.
He went to Gethsemane and waited for his Accusers in prayerful obedience.
He asked the Father if there might be another way.
He went willingly when they came for him.
He endured and accomplished the purpose for which he was born.
He did *all* his Father's will.

*Matthew 5:2-12*

*2 And he opened his mouth and taught them, saying: 3 "Blessed are the poor in spirit, for theirs is the kingdom of heaven. 4 "Blessed are those who mourn, for they shall be comforted. 5 "Blessed are the meek, for they shall inherit the earth. 6 "Blessed are those who hunger and thirst for righteousness, for they shall be satisfied. 7 "Blessed are the merciful, for they shall receive mercy. 8 "Blessed are the pure in heart, for they shall see God. 9 "Blessed are the peacemakers, for they shall be called sons of God. 10 "Blessed are those who are persecuted for righteousness' sake, for theirs is the kingdom of heaven. 11 "Blessed are you when others revile you and persecute you and utter all kinds of evil against you falsely on my account. 12 Rejoice and be glad, for your reward is great in heaven, for so they persecuted the prophets who were before you.*

Like Jesus, learn to only say and do what the Father gives you to say and do! As we learn to walk in his attitudes and develop the various relational disciplines, we will see and hear better and better - with the help and encouragement of the Holy Spirit. More and more, better and better (2 Corinthians 3:18). We can. We can! *Love* will help you in this.

Have you noticed that Jesus' attitudes in the Beatitudes build upon one another even as they promise blessing? If we will consider the order of his promises to bless, we may also see that there is a progression as we *become like him in our attitudes…*

*Jesus' Attitudes: The Attitudes to "Be In"*

- *Be poor in spirit, be humble, don't think so much about yourself!*
- *When you mourn, be comforted by a Big Picture understanding of why you are here, that life is short and that eternity with God awaits.*
- *Be meek: gentleness as a way of life.*
- *Hunger and thirst for righteousness. Pray as Jesus taught us to pray: Give us justice against our adversaries, O God, and send your laborers to them that they repent and come into right relationship with you. Do your works in us and make us effective laborers, too! Flow your gentle righteousness through us to others and accomplish your will.*
- *Be merciful, and receive mercy!*
- *Be pure in heart, overcome the temptations of anger.*
- *Be a peacemaker, child of God!*
- *When you are persecuted for righteousness' sake, as God flows his gentle righteousness through you to others; when others revile you and persecute you and utter all kinds of evil against you falsely on his account; rejoice and be glad, for your reward is great in heaven, for so they persecuted the prophets who were before you!*

One with him, *becoming* like Jesus, we will only want to say and do what the Father makes known to us. Participating with him *in his will* as we live in Jesus' attitudes.

Made in his image, he very much desires that we would be creative like he is creative. We are not to be robots simply following his commands, but rather *creative participants in conversational collaboration* with him in the administration and operation of his kingdom. Consider our first creative participation with him:

*Genesis 2:19-20*

*19 Now out of the ground the Lord God had formed every beast of the field and every bird of the heavens and brought them to the man to see what he would call them. And whatever the man called every living creature, that was its name. 20 The man gave names to all livestock and to the birds of the heavens and to every beast of the field...*

Consider also the fall of wicked King Ahab:

*1 Kings 16:33*

*"[King Ahab] did more to provoke the Lord, the God of Israel, to anger than all the kings of Israel who were before him".*

God had made a decision to deliver his people from King Ahab's evil, but he brought the *creation of how* to the members of his divine kingdom:

*1 Kings 22:19-23*

*19 And Micaiah said, "Therefore hear the word of the Lord: I saw*
*the Lord sitting on his throne, and <u>all the host of heaven</u> standing beside him*
*on his right hand and on his left; 20 and the Lord said, 'Who will entice Ahab,*
*that he may go up and fall at Ramoth-gilead?' And one said one thing, and*
*another said another. 21 Then a spirit came forward and stood before*
*the Lord, saying, 'I will entice him.' 22 <u>And the Lord said to him, 'By what</u>*
*<u>means?'</u> And he said, 'I will go out, and will be a lying spirit in the mouth of all*
*his prophets.' And he said, 'You are to entice him, and you shall succeed; go*
*out and do so.' 23 Now therefore behold, the Lord has put a lying spirit in the*
*mouth of all these your prophets; the Lord has declared disaster for you."*

*1 Kings 22:37-38*

*37 So the king died, and was brought to Samaria. And they buried the king in*
*Samaria. 38 And they washed the chariot by the pool of Samaria, and the dogs*
*licked up his blood, and the prostitutes washed themselves in it,*
*according to the word of the Lord that he had spoken.*

They participated with him then, and later the disciples participated with him as well. Jesus didn't do it alone:

*Mark 6:34-44*

*34 When he went ashore he saw a great crowd, and he had compassion on them, because they were like sheep without a shepherd. And he began to teach them many things. 35 And when it grew late, his disciples came to him and said, "This is a desolate place, and the hour is now late. 36 Send them away to go into the surrounding countryside and villages and buy themselves something to eat." 37 But he answered them, "You give them something to eat." And they said to him, "Shall we go and buy two hundred denarii worth of bread and give it to them to eat?" 38 And he said to them, "How many loaves do you have? Go and see." And when they had found out, they said, "Five, and two fish." 39 Then he commanded them all to sit down in groups on the green grass. 40 So they sat down in groups, by hundreds and by fifties. 41 And taking the five loaves and the two fish, he looked up to heaven and said a blessing and broke the loaves and gave them to the disciples to set before the people. And he divided the two fish among them all. 42 And they all ate and were satisfied. 43 And they took up twelve baskets full of broken pieces and of the fish. 44 And those who ate the loaves were five thousand men.*

If we will *participate* with him on earth as it is in heaven *now*, we will also participate with him on the *new* earth after he comes again:

*Matthew 19:28-29*

*28 Jesus said to them, "Truly, I say to you, in the new world, when the Son of Man will sit on his glorious throne, you who have followed me will also sit on twelve thrones, judging the twelve tribes of Israel. 29 And everyone who has left houses or brothers or sisters or father or mother or children or lands, for my name's sake, will receive a hundredfold and will inherit eternal life.*

*1 Corinthians 6:2-3a*

*2 Or do you not know that the saints will judge the world? And if the world is to be judged by you, are you incompetent to try trivial cases? 3 Do you not know that we are to judge angels?*

*2 Timothy 2:12*

*if we endure, we will also reign with him; if we deny him, he also will deny us;*

*Revelation 2:26*
*The one who conquers and who keeps my works until the end, to him I will give authority over the nations,*

*Revelation 3:21*
*The one who conquers, I will grant him to sit with me on my throne, as I also conquered and sat down with my Father on his throne.*

*Revelation 20:6*
*6 Blessed and holy is the one who shares in the first resurrection! Over such the second death has no power, but they will be priests of God and of Christ, and they will reign with him for a thousand years.*

*Revelation 21:1*
*Then I saw a new heaven and a new earth, for the first heaven and the first earth had passed away, and the sea was no more.*

*Revelation 22:5*
*And night will be no more. They will need no light of lamp or sun, for the Lord God will be their light, and they will reign forever and ever.*

****************

While we will certainly err along the way, God is Gentle as he points out the better way, always treating us with fruit of the Spirit: Love, Joy, Peace, Patience, Kindness, Goodness, Perseverance, Gentleness and Self-Control. As he models these for us, we learn to model them for others.

As he lives in us and leads us into the abundant life, we will find Joy and Peace that surpass all understanding. As we learn that his ways are better than our ways, *what we will want will become what he wants us to want*. He will show us how what he wants us to want will bring us the best life we could possibly live.

He did this for his *talmidim* over a period of three years. Present with them, he taught them his character, his attributes, his attitudes, how to overcome their destructive passions and desires and how to live by the power of his Presence. Despite whatever their life circumstances were or would be, they found his promise of Joy in him to be true. He molded and shaped their character day by day and rooted it into them.

In the *Life* section, we learned that it is really quite simple to understand what it means to be a true Christ Follower. Though it is quite a difficult thing to live out each day, what we *are* to be doing has some very simple reference points. It's time to once again return to *living lives pleasing to God*. The last page of the *Life* section sums up *how* for us:

## ***True talmidim will evidence:***

- Dominion over the earth, but not over people. (Genesis 1:26-30)
  - Give us a king. (1 Samuel 8:4-22)
  - Jesus said it shall not be so among you. (Mark 10:42-45)
- The Ten Commandments (Exodus 20:3-17)
- Love the Lord your God with all your heart, soul, mind and strength, your neighbor as yourself and one another as I have loved you. (Mark 12:30-31, John 13:34-35)
- "Love" active in service. (John 12:26, Mark 9:35, Mark 10:45, Galatians 5:13, Matthew 20:26-27, 1 Samuel 12:24)
- Hearts after the Father in attitudes consistent with the Beatitudes: Jesus' attitudes. (Matthew 5:2-12)
- Fruit of the Spirit language and actions. (Galatians 5:22-24)
- The Unity, character and attributes of John 17.
- Knowing God's voice and be following *Him*. (John 10:27)
- Creative collaboration and participation in accomplishing the will of the Father. (Genesis 2:19-20, 1 Kings 22:19-23 and Mark 6:34-44)
- Only saying and doing what the Father gives them to say and do. (John 5:19, John 12:49-50, John 14:10)
- The elimination of Anger, Judgement, Condemnation, Hierarchy and Manipulate To Control behaviors from their lives. (Romans 1:28-32, Colossians 3:1-17, Galatians 5:13-26, John 17)
- The overcoming of the temptations and desires of the flesh, their sacrifice nothing compared to Jesus' sacrifice on our behalf. (Romans 1:18-32, Colossians 3:1-17, Galatians 5:13-26, Leviticus 18, Ephesians 5:1-21, James 4:1-12, 1 Peter 2:11-12, Ephesians 2:1-7, 1 John 2:3-6)
- That they are *becoming* mature and effective laborers more and more: the 12, the 70 and the 500.

# Chapter Two

## Hallowed Be Thy Presence

As in the *Life* section, capital letters are used for the personification of various characteristics and behaviors so as to identify them with God or his Enemies.

Jesus' entire ministry taught that one word: Love. The problem is that we all want to define that word ourselves, so he spent three years defining it for us with his talmidim - giving us a *living* testimony of what *love in action* looks like.

When Jesus' talmidim asked him to teach them how to pray, what he gave them was the most all-encompassing prayer that could be prayed. All of the law, the prophets and the entire Old Testament, may be summed up in the two all-encompassing commandments: "Love the Lord your God with all of your heart, with all of your soul, with all of your mind and with all of your strength." and "Love your neighbor as yourself." Similarly, I believe that this prayer Jesus taught us sums up all of the *essential* content that we might *pray* for the whole world and for our *becoming* as talmidim.

*By the time he gave them this prayer, he had already spent three years teaching them the associated lessons multiple times and in multiple ways. As we will see, each section of this prayer therefore served as a reminding reference of the lessons previously learned for whatever situation they could ever find themselves in. Having been prepared by Jesus' teaching and training, and armed with this brief prayer on their hearts, they would be able to quickly remember and agree with the Father's will in any moment, in any Life situation, and be able to humbly respond by the leading and power of the Holy Spirit - in the attitudes of the Beatitudes (Jesus' attitudes) with fruit of the Spirit language and actions - always and everywhere. That the Father's will be done on earth as it is in heaven.*

In John 17, Jesus clearly states that, during the three years with his talmidim, he manifested in them (established, engrained, developed, activated and made real) *the character and attributes of God (personal holiness).* That was before Pentecost and their receiving of the Holy Spirit within them! He went on to say that, *him in us and us in him*, all may grow to manifest them and that these are essential behaviors if we are to accomplish his will for us – that his kingdom come (be established) and will be done on (the whole) earth as it is in heaven *for the making of talmidim* of all nations.

If they could manifest the character and attributes of God *without* yet having received the Holy Spirit, we can surely do so *with* the Holy Spirit. Jesus asked our Father for this during that same prayer.

At Pentecost, those gathered went from having *learned* how to *become* like their rabbi Jesus (operating in the character and attributes Jesus established in them) while Jesus was *with them* - to then having the Presence of the Spirit of the Living God *in them. Personal holiness* is now more fully available and attainable through what Jesus taught us, by the power of the Holy Spirit and with the Father in us doing his works!

*1 Corinthians 6:19*
*Or do you not know that your body is a temple of the Holy Spirit within you, whom you have from God?*

*John 14:10*
*Do you not believe that I am in the Father and the Father is in me? The words that I say to you I do not speak on my own authority, but the Father who dwells in me does his works.*

Like God, our reputation comes from our actions. Like me, I suspect your reputation has not always been sterling with everyone. But now, operating *in* his name, that is, *in* the power of his Presence, *him in us and us in him*, we may better reflect his character and attributes to those around us if we will only *allow him* to manifest them in us. By so doing, he will establish them, engrain them, develop them, activate them and make them real in us (2 Corinthians 3:18 and Romans 8:29: little by little, success by success, glory by glory; conformed to the image of his Son).

****************

Just as the enormous depth of the practical application of the two love commandments may be found in the scriptures, the enormous depth of the content of the prayers he taught us to pray may also be found there. For more than 30 years I have been asking that I be taught how to pray. What I have learned is that this particular prayer, when expanded upon through examination of the associated lessons in scripture, explains the attitudes, character and attributes that we, his talmidim, will share *as one with him* if we are to *creatively collaborate and participate* in the will of the Father.

As I researched the attitudes, character and attributes of Adonai, what I found was a long list of "names", the meanings of which actually *describe* his character and attributes. Occasionally, some of these names also speak of the *reputation* he carries.

Significantly, and as was discussed in greater detail in the *Life* section, "name", was originally used to describe his Presence, *including* his character, attributes and reputation.

*Outside of Eden, God would just show up in supernatural ways. As they sensed his presence and experienced his activity supernaturally, they would talk about his "panim", the Hebrew word meaning "presence". Eventually, they decided they needed to name "the panim". (You probably remember that he didn't actually give them his name until much much later.) So as they considered, they called him Hashem, capital H. But why Hashem? Because in the Hebrew language "shem" means "name", and "Ha" is a way of adding an honorific to the word.*

*So Hashem was what they called God as they felt his presence and "heard" from him, but could not see him. They continued to call him Hashem (The Presence) even after he told them his name (Yahweh) because they felt it may be insulting to him to say his name aloud. The Hebrew people continue to use Hashem as a "name" for God in their daily prayers to this day.*

*The point of all of this is that, in Hebrew, Hashem refers to "The Presence" of God as he expresses his character, attributes and reputation for reliable activity on our behalf.*

*Almost always, the English word "name" found in our bibles is a mistranslation of its etymology from panim to shem to Hashem. So, when we talk of asking in his "name", what we are really speaking of is asking while in his Presence, thankful for his reliable reputation and activity on our behalf - and for the development of his character and attributes in us more and more.*

*When you read scripture, it will be far more meaningful if you will watch to see whether the meaning of "name" is "name", or if it would be more appropriate to substitute "Presence", "the presence", "the character and attributes", "in the power of the presence", "in the power of the presence and in the character and attributes" or another contextually appropriate phrase. Occasionally, "reputation" will be most appropriate.*

As was more thoroughly described in the *Life* section, he wants more than to just be in our presence, or us in his. What he wants is what has been available to us since Pentecost: his relational Presence at work *in us, through us and with us as members of the Family of God*. In so doing, rivers of living water will *flow out of us* by the power of the Spirit as we *participate with him for the benefit of the people around us*. Notice, too, that he says it flows from our hearts, not our minds. Our *hearts* after his.

*John 7:37-39*

*37 On the last day of the feast, the great day, Jesus stood up and cried out, "If anyone thirsts, let him come to me and drink. 38 Whoever believes in me, as the Scripture has said, '<u>Out of his heart will flow rivers of living water</u>.'" 39 Now this he said about the Spirit, whom those who believed in him were to receive, for as yet the Spirit had not been given, because Jesus was not yet glorified.*

In him, we are *willing participants* in the administration of his kingdom as he *flows through us* to bring it on earth as it is in heaven. As was more fully described in the *Life* section, he desires that we be *creative* with him insofar as *how* his will might best be accomplished. He does not desire robots following orders. Rather, made as his *imager*, it is his joy that we might creatively imagine ways and means for accomplishment with him: *willing participants in creative collaboration*.

****************

*In the Lord's Prayer, the prayer Jesus taught us to pray, doesn't "Presence" make more sense than "name"? Our Father in heaven, hallowed be your presence! Your kingdom come, your will be done!*

After all, it is the power of his presence working in us that strengthens us to overcome the difficulties of living in this world. We are not to take this world on alone. Our Father in heaven, thank you for your presence!

Present *together*, God's desire is to lead us through each day in one-ness with him, taught by him, to grow us to reflect his character and attributes to others more and more, little by little, success by success, glory by glory (2 Corinthians 3:18); conformed to the image of his Son (Romans 8:29), that none should perish (2 Peter 3:9). Jesus asked our Father for this in his lengthy John 17 prayer:

*John 17:20-21*

*20 "I do not ask for these only, but <u>also for those who will believe in me</u>*
*through their word, 21 that they may all be one, just as you, Father,*
*are in me, and I in you, that they also may be in us, so that*
*the world may believe that you have sent me.*

*Colossians 3:17*

*17 And whatever you do, in word or deed, <u>do everything in the name (in the</u>*
*<u>power of the Presence, character & attributes) of the Lord Jesus,</u>*
*giving thanks to God the Father through him.*

We are Present *together*, him in us and us in him. Any "not fruit of the Spirit" behavior is "not him", "not love". We are to be always listening for his voice, asking him to help us monitor our behavior in order that, more and more, we will love wholly and love only, doing everything *with* him, in the power of his Presence, consistent with the character & attributes of the Father as seen in the life and attitudes of our Lord Jesus, giving thanks to God the Father through him. This requires the bending of our will to his - including the aligning of our hearts, souls and minds – that he manifest himself to us, establishing himself *in* us. One with him, he will regenerate our hearts and fill us with his Spirit, speak to our spirit, and lead our minds perfectly. That we have the mind of Christ, his attitudes, character and attributes, and hearts after the Father's.

He is the One who will be helping always. Sometimes whispering it and sometimes shouting it, he says, "Look how special you are! I made you for a purpose, with passion and giftedness to help you know with great certainty! Be one with me, your heart fully after my heart! Listen to my Spirit in your spirit that your mind may know how to proceed! Love, risk rejection, give selflessly!

My Spirit is in you, I am teaching you to give, for my supply will replenish you! Love! Serve! Reconcile! My sheep know my voice and follow me! Learn my ways that you may have a joyful life, and have it abundantly! Listen, look and do as I did, the Father accomplishing his Works within me!"

****************

The original meaning for the Hebrew word translated into English for us as prayer, is *conversational worship*. As *willing participants in creative collaboration*, prayer is our way of telling him what is on our minds as we simultaneously praise him and ask him to share his heart and his will for us in it. Being creative about it with him, we ask for clarity, wisdom and his leading as to how we might best participate with him in doing it. Sometimes our participation will be through words or actions, and sometimes it will be through prayers of agreement with him for it - as he leads *others* to do it.

Though we cannot see the Father, Son or Holy Spirit, when we pray let us imagine that we are face to face with *Them* and looking *Them* in the eye. (Forgive me for using *Them* to make my point. Adonai is One!) If we will do this, it will be harder to pray selfishly and easier to ask to understand his will.

Then, in his *Presence* (in his *name*), we will ask for what is *his* will, in *his* character, consistent with *his* reputation, by the power of *his* Presence in us, joyful that we are blessed to be *participating in it with him. Agreeing* with him for *his* will and asking him in this way, we may be *confident*:

*Psalm 124:8*

*Our help is in the name (Presence) of the Lord, who made heaven and earth.*

*Hebrews 4:14-16*

*14 Since then we have a great high priest who has passed through the heavens, Jesus, the Son of God, let us hold fast our confession. 15 For we do not have a high priest who is unable to sympathize with our weaknesses, but one who in every respect has been tempted as we are, yet without sin. 16 Let us then with confidence draw near to the throne of grace, that we may receive mercy and find grace to help in time of need.*

The Catholics start and end their prayers with the Sign of the Cross saying, "In the name of the Father and of the Son and of the Holy Spirit." It has been helpful for me to revise this, acknowledging and reminding myself that I am *in the Presence* of the Father, and of the Son and of the Holy Spirit. Then, spiritually face-to-face, I am better able to be present myself for dialogue with Adonai our triune God. Better able to listen, I am more likely to be willing, remembering that it is *his* will and Direction that I am asking for.

If you will join me in this, it will therefore more and more be his will that *we* are asking for, to know and agree with and desire to do – for we know that our Joy will be full as *we* participate in his will *with* him - believing and trusting that his way is better than our way, our hearts after his, desiring only *his* will.

*1 John 5:14-15 NASB*
*14 This is the confidence which we have before Him, that, if we ask anything according to His will, He hears us. 15 And if we know that He hears us in whatever we ask, we know that we have the requests which we have asked from Him.*

# Chapter Three

## If We Ask Anything According To His Will, He Hears Us

*1 John 5:14-15 NASB*
*14 This is the confidence which we have before Him, that, if we ask anything according to His will, He hears us. 15 And if we know that He hears us in whatever we ask, we know that we have the requests which we have asked from Him.*

*John 14:12-14*
*12 "Truly, truly, I say to you, whoever believes in me will also do the works that I do; and greater works than these will he do, because I am going to the Father. 13 Whatever you ask in my name (in the power of my Presence, in my character, consistent with my reputation and in agreement for the Father's will), this I will do, that the Father may be glorified in the Son. 14 If you ask me anything in my name (in the power of my Presence, in my character, consistent with my reputation and in agreement for the Father's will), I will do it.*

*John 14:26*
*But the Helper, the Holy Spirit, whom the Father will send in my name (with the power of my Presence, in my character, consistent with my reputation and in agreement with the Father's will), he will teach you all things and bring to your remembrance all that I have said to you.*

*John 15:16*
*You did not choose me, but I chose you and appointed you that you should go and bear fruit and that your fruit should abide, so that whatever you ask the Father in my name (in the power of my Presence, in my character, consistent with my reputation and in agreement for the Father's will), he may give it to you.*

*John 16:23*
*In that day you will ask nothing of me. Truly, truly, I say to you, whatever you ask of the Father in my name (in the power of my Presence, in my character, consistent with my reputation and in agreement for the Father's will), he will give it to you.*

*John 16:24*
*Until now you have asked nothing in my name (in the power of my Presence, in my character, consistent with my reputation and in agreement for the Father's will). Ask, and you will receive, that your joy may be full.*

Many end their prayers, "In Jesus' name. Amen" because of the above references (John 14:12-14, John 14:26, John 15:16, John 16:23, John 16:24, and Mark 11:23-25 that is used on the next page) and because our teachers have modeled it. But often it sounds more like an incantation of some sort to get what we want, believing that God must give it to us because we used the magic words and asked *in his name*. I frequently see that it is being said in some degree of ignorance of its meaning, though intentions may be good. Following in the error of what our church teachers have taught us to say, and them theirs, we have lost our understanding over time. Just because we say *in his name*, or *in Jesus' name*, we cannot expect our requests to be done for us. Jesus knew that this day of mistaken understanding would come, and he spoke of it:

*John 16:26*
*In that day you will ask in my name, and I do **not** say to you that I will ask the Father on your behalf;*

*James 4:2b-3*
*2b… You do not have, because you do not ask. 3 You ask and do not receive, because you ask wrongly, to spend it on your passions.*

Mistranslations of the ancient Hebrew have led us to us to the translation "name" and therefore our ignorance of its true meaning as "presence". The NASB is helpful for us here, and is in agreement with the totality and context of the original scripture:

*1 John 5:14-15 NASB*
*14 This is the confidence which we have before Him, that, if we ask anything according to His will, He hears us. 15 And if we know that He hears us in whatever we ask, we know that we have the requests which we have asked from Him.*

*Unfortunately, ending our prayers "in the name of Jesus" has become a sort of incantation that has come about due to mistranslations in our Bibles.*

We would be better off ending our prayers like Jesus did at Gethsemane before he willingly went off to die, *having received confirmation of the Father's will there*. Why not finish with something like, "Father, desiring to participate with you in making talmidim of all nations and in the establishment of your kingdom on earth as it is in heaven, we have asked these things because you say that we may ask. Now, here in your Presence, we have asked them *in our best understanding* of your will. But not our will, yours be done."

So, when we say that we are praying *in his name (in his presence)*, it must be that we are *in full agreement* that it be *his* will, *his* way, and that we desire to *follow after him* in *that* will, desiring that *more and more* we will be walking in Jesus' *attitudes* and asking *in his character,* with *behavior* consistent with *his* reputation, trusting that *he will do it through us as we participate in it with him*. Because he is the one who placed the desire for us to ask it in our hearts in the first place, *our hearts after his*. *Joy* is ours knowing that he will do what is best, and we thrill to see how he will bring it to pass!

*As he lives in us and leads us into the abundant life, we will find Joy and Peace that surpass all understanding. As we learn that his ways are better than our ways, <u>what we will want will more and more become what he wants us to want</u>. In this way, we will <u>begin</u> our prayers acknowledging his Presence, agreeing for <u>his</u> will, learning to ask "in his presence" <u>for what he wants us to be asking for</u>! In the attitudes, character and attributes of Jesus, consistent with the reputation of the Father, in and for <u>the Father's</u> will.*
*No more incantations!*

****************

*1 John 5:14-15 NASB*
*14 This is the confidence which we have before Him, that, if we ask anything <u>according to His will</u>, He hears us. 15 And if we know that <u>He hears us</u> in whatever we ask, <u>we know that we have</u> the requests which we have asked from Him.*

*Mark 11:23-25*

*23 Truly, I say to you, whoever says to this mountain, 'Be taken up and thrown into the sea,' and does not doubt in his heart, but believes that what he says will come to pass, it will be done for him. 24 Therefore I tell you, whatever you ask in prayer, believe that you have received it (are receiving it), and it will be yours. 25 And whenever you stand praying, forgive, if you have anything against anyone, so that your Father also who is in heaven may forgive you your trespasses. 26 But if you do not forgive, neither will your Father who is in heaven forgive your trespasses."*

Please note that some manuscripts have translated it "have received it" and others have translated it "are receiving it". Nonetheless, *he* is the one doing it so we *have received* it, *are receiving* it, or *will be receiving* it in his timing - according to his will. Jesus asked the Father that we be one as he is one. It has not yet come to pass, but it *is* in the process of occurring. *He is causing what as of yet has not been fully caused.*

Given what we learned in the *Life* section about Jesus only saying and doing what the Father told him, it is important to recognize that *what Jesus asked for, received and was receiving*, was *always* in alignment with the Father's will. While Jesus believes without a doubt that the Father's kingdom will come and his will *will* be done, he is *only in the process of receiving it*. And so are we.

*John 17:20-23*

*20 "I do not ask for these only, but also for those who will believe in me through their word, 21 that they may all be one, just as you, Father, are in me, and I in you, that they also may be in us, so that the world may believe that you have sent me. 22 The glory that you have given me I have given to them, that they may be one even as we are one, 23 I in them and you in me, that they may become perfectly one, so that the world may know that you sent me and loved them even as you loved me.*

His kingdom *is* coming, his will *is* in the process of being accomplished. We *are* participating with him to manifest and establish his kingdom on earth - in the hearts, souls and minds of people - as it is in heaven. He wants us to agree with him that it be done – and believe that we *are* in the process of receiving it – according to the Father's timing.

It is important to realize that in stating our agreement with him regarding his kingdom and will, we are somehow *participating with him to cause that which has not yet been caused, release that which has not yet been released and/or fulfill that which is in the process of being fulfilled.*

He asks us to ask, so we ask - because that is how he wants it. We don't know why he does it this way, but he does. Jesus told us to ask this way when he taught us how to pray. Must we understand how and why it is this way? I think not, but that it *is* this way is apparent from the words he taught us to *use*.

*We are collaborators co-operating, him in us spiritually and us in him spiritually, with us in the physical creatively participating with him to bring the spiritual into earthly manifestation. Establishing his kingdom on earth as it is in heaven - in people - his will being done: that all might come to know him, love him and join him, and thereby enter into the Family of God.*
*That none should perish.*

It is similarly so regarding him telling us to pray earnestly to the Lord of the harvest to send laborers:

*Matthew 9;35-38*

*35 And Jesus went throughout all the cities and villages, teaching in their synagogues and proclaiming the gospel of the kingdom and healing every disease and every affliction. 36 When he saw the crowds, he had compassion for them, because they were harassed and helpless, like sheep without a shepherd. 37 Then he said to his disciples, "The harvest is plentiful, but the laborers are few; 38 therefore pray earnestly to the Lord of the harvest to send out laborers into his harvest."*

As well, we are to be persistent in these prayers:

*Luke 18:1-8*

*1 And he told them a parable to the effect that they ought always to pray and not lose heart. 2 He said, "In a certain city there was a judge who neither feared God nor respected man. 3 And there was a widow in that city who kept coming to him and saying, 'Give me justice against my adversary.' 4 For a while he refused, but afterward he said to himself, 'Though I neither fear God nor respect man, 5 yet because this widow keeps bothering me, I will give her justice, so that she will not beat me down by her continual coming.'" 6 And the*

*Lord said, "Hear what the unrighteous judge says. 7 And will not God give justice to his elect, who cry to him day and night? Will he delay long over them? 8 I tell you, he will give justice to them speedily. Nevertheless, when the Son of Man comes, will he find faith on earth?"*

What happens when we ask the things that he has told us to ask? Why does it matter to him that we ask them? How does he respond when we do? Why does it work this way? I do not know. But ask! And *in remembrance of him only saying what the Father gave him to say and only doing what the Father gave him to do*, be one who follows it up with *love in action.*

By the time that they asked him to teach them how to pray, he had already told them a few other things that a talmid will desire and be conversationally asking of God. Jesus specifically told them (and us) to pray these 4 prayers:

1. Luke 18:1-8 *Persevere in asking for justice against our adversaries.*
2. Matthew 5:43-46 *Love your enemies - pray for those who persecute you*
3. Matthew 9:35-38 *pray earnestly to the Lord of the harvest to send out laborers into his harvest.*
4. Matthew 6:9-14 *Pray then like this: Our Father in heaven, hallowed be your name. Your kingdom come, your will be done...*

As we persevere in asking God for people every day, we must remember the true meaning of the word *prayer* in the original Hebrew: conversational worship. When we contemplate the depth of these 4 prayers together, remembering to listen and praise as well, he will more and more give us hearts after himself and a better comprehension of his ways. This is sanctification, his refinement of us, that we will more and more gain hearts after the Father and the mind and attitudes of Christ.

I am in *conversational worship* with the Father, Son and Holy Spirit throughout each day, often asking him for the people I know and the populations of this world many times throughout the day. Although this is the order I've given them to you in, I change up the order of these 4 prayers all the time:

*Dear God,*
*Give us justice against our adversaries. Send Your laborers and draw them into Your harvest. Bind and loose according to Your will. May they repent, turn*

*to You, be healed and come into right relationship with You. That they live the abundant life You have in mind for them both here and eternally.*

*Make us effective laborers, O God, and send us, too. Lead us into repentance, too. Refine us, strengthen us and sanctify us that our hearts be fully after Yours and accomplish all Your will for us.*

*Deliver us from evil, and deliver us from the evil we would do if we were to enter into the temptations around us. Forgive us when we fail You, O God, and use these to train us up in preparation against future temptations. Recognizing Your forgiveness for us, lead us that we learn to forgive others in the same way You forgive: without shaming, but in Gentleness with Patience, Kindness, Goodness, Perseverance and Self-Control.*

*May all the people of the world be fed today. Not just with food and water, but with the filling of Your Spirit. That they become faithful followers accomplishing Your will for them.*

*Thank You that Your kingdom is in the process of coming across the whole world. Accomplish Your will today, on earth as it is in heaven! Hallowed and glorious is Your presence! There is no one like You. You are our Father! You are preparing our place with You for all eternity! Hallelujah! All praise and glory and honor are Yours forever and ever, amen!*

Such a brief and simple prayer. Yet it encompasses the whole world!

*Genesis 15:6*
*And he believed the Lord, and <u>he counted it to him as righteousness</u>.*

*James 5:16*
*Therefore confess your sins to each other and pray for each other so that you may be healed. <u>The prayer of a righteous person is powerful and effective</u>.*

*Psalm 5:8*
*<u>Lead me, O Lord, in your righteousness</u> because of my enemies;*
*make your way straight before me.*

*Deuteronomy 6:25*
*And <u>it will be righteousness for us</u>, if we are careful to do all this commandment before the Lord our God, as he has commanded us.'*

*Isaiah 60:17*

*Instead of bronze I will bring gold, and instead of iron I will bring silver; instead of wood, bronze, instead of stones, iron. I will make your overseers peace and your taskmasters righteousness.*

*Matthew 6:33*

*But seek first the kingdom of God and his righteousness, and all these things will be added to you.*

Therefore, ask him to flow *his righteousness* through you in your *becoming* – that your prayers be powerful and effective!

# *Chapter Four*

## Which Comes First?

The scripture in the preceding chapter (John 14:12-14, John 14:26, John 15:16, John 16:23, John 16:24 and Mark 11:23-25) are some of the so called "proof texts" for those who have been Deceived into believing that we have the Power and Authority to make things happen on our own – because we think it would be *good* and believe that we have been *given the right*. But, if so, we are *leaning on our own understanding*, not the totality of the scriptures - and are at risk of being the workers of lawlessness who will be told to depart from him.

*Matthew 7:22-23*
*"On that day many will say to me, 'Lord, Lord, did we not prophesy in your name, and cast out demons in your name, and do many mighty works in your name?' And then will I declare to them, 'I never knew you; depart from me, you workers of lawlessness.'"*

Which comes first? "I only say and do as the Father tells me?" Or, "Ask anything in my name and you will receive it?" The first precedes the second.

If we are *becoming* just like our rabbi Jesus, if we are *one with him*, our *hearts* after the Father's, then we focus ourselves on God's will and doing *it*. One with him, in his Presence, in his character and according to his attributes – we will be asking for what he wants us to ask for – and we will surely *receive it* or *be receiving* it.

*Romans 8:26*
*Likewise, the Spirit helps us in our weakness. For we do not know what to pray for as we ought, but the Spirit himself intercedes for us with groanings too deep for words.*

*1 John 5:14-15 NASB*
*14 This is the confidence which we have before Him, that, if we ask anything according to His will, He hears us. 15 And if we know that He hears us in whatever we ask, we know that we have the requests which we have asked from Him.*

Because we believe him for what his Spirit is telling our spirit to ask for, *it will come to pass*. It will. If Adonai tells us to throw this mountain into the sea *now*, it will be done by him *now* through the manifestation of his power *flowing through* us - *now*! Otherwise, though we may hope for something *now*, it may be that his will is that it occur in the future, and so *it is in the process* of being done by the manifestation of his power *as it is flowing now and will flow in the future*.

One with him, he is the Vine, we are the branches. We can do nothing worthwhile without him. *For* him is under our power.

*John 16:26*

*In that day you will ask in my name, and I do **not** say to you that I will ask the Father on your behalf;*

*James 4:2b-3*

*2b... You do not have, because you do not ask. 3 You ask and do not receive, because you ask wrongly, to spend it on your passions.*

*With* him is under his.

*Psalm 127:1-2*

*1 Unless the Lord builds the house, those who build it labor in vain. Unless the Lord watches over the city, the watchman stays awake in vain. 2 It is in vain that you rise up early and go late to rest, eating the bread of anxious toil; for he gives to his beloved sleep.*

*John 15:1-5*

*4 Abide in me, and I in you. As the branch cannot bear fruit by itself, unless it abides in the vine, neither can you, unless you abide in me. 5 I am the vine; you are the branches. Whoever abides in me and I in him, he it is that bears much fruit, for apart from me you can do nothing.*

So, when we have an idea, *creating* as he made us to do, we lift it up to him and ask if it was prompted *by* him. *Continuing* to ask him about it, we praise him for the opportunity to creatively *participate* in it with him, and ask him what else we need to know about it. Are there others that he has introduced us to previously that might be useful in clarification, and in the doing of it?

Our hearts after his. Our ways desiring his. Our words and actions desiring alignment with him and his Wisdom, we wait Patiently on *his timing* before initiating action. If the time is *not yet*, be confident that he will bring more clarity as his timing approaches. And *when* the time is right, have faith that it will be accomplished.

*2 Peter 3:9*
*The Lord is not slow to fulfill his promise as some count slowness, but is patient toward you, not wishing that any should perish, but that all should reach repentance.*

*Mark 13:32*
*"But concerning that day or that hour, no one knows, not even the angels in heaven, nor the Son, but only the Father.*

*Matthew 24:36*
*"But concerning that day and hour no one knows, not even the angels of heaven, nor the Son, but the Father only.*

*If we will grow as talmidim and participate with him in the making of more talmidim, we must similarly open ourselves up to his fruit of the Spirit ways of teaching and training. The prayers Jesus told us to pray are constant reminders to walk in his attitudes, our hearts after the Father and his will, utilizing fruit of the Spirit language and actions always and everywhere – that we produce fruit of the Spirit.*

# *Chapter Five*

## The Wise, The Fool And The Corrupt

Over the last two thousand plus years, the followers of Jesus have been relating how Jesus came to inform us of God's love for us, of our opportunity to choose a relationship with him that will survive our earthly death, and the availability of an afterlife of eternal joy in his Presence.

They share that Jesus warned that a portion of the religious leaders of their day had been borne of a *Corrupt* lineage, intent upon using their positions for personal advancement and the Control and Direction of people.

He shared that another portion of the religious leaders of their day were simply well-intentioned *Fools*, unaware of the harm they were bringing upon themselves and others by their ignorance.

He went on to explain a third portion of the people who he called *Wise*, their wisdom coming from their understanding of the ways of God. He advised that the *Wise* could be counted upon to *become wise and effective leaders* in the service of the people.

For all of our benefit, he further explained how we might tell the difference between the *Corrupt*, the *Fool* and the *Wise*: through the behaviors which set them apart. People of these three types are identified in detail throughout Old Testament scripture. Referencing fruit of the Spirit language and actions (Galatians 5:22-23) in the attitudes of the Beatitudes (Matthew 5:2-12), *Life* describes just how easy it is to tell the difference (Galatians 5:17-21, Colossians 3:5-17) and avoid their Divisive influence.

Even now leaders still come from portions of all three; whether they be church leaders, business leaders, family leaders or our leaders in governance: the *Wise*, the *Fool* and the *Corrupt*.

The Enemy is convincing the Fool and the Corrupt to war against us so that we might pass Foolishness and Corruption down to the 3rd and 4th generation of our children (Exodus 20:5-6, Numbers 14:18, Isaiah 65:6-7, Jeremiah 32:18-19), so that they can be passed down to their children, too. The Enemy wants to interrupt the passing down of any Wisdom so that *Fools* may instead pass down ignorance, grow *Corruption* and block vision – so that the people perish (KJV Proverbs 29:18 Where there is no vision the people perish).

Pray for the children! Caught up in the physical and focused upon getting their worldly wants, without *Wisdom* they will be out of touch with the Spiritual. Short-sighted, they will never even realize that they are entangled in the war for souls happening all around them – and the disintegration of families and nations.

The consequences of our actions are being allowed to play out:

*Romans 1:28-32*

*28 And since they did not see fit to acknowledge God, God gave them up to a*
*debased mind to do what ought not to be done. 29 They were filled with all*
*manner of unrighteousness, evil, covetousness, malice. They are full of envy,*
*murder, strife, deceit, maliciousness. They are gossips, 30 slanderers, haters of*
*God, insolent, haughty, boastful, inventors of evil, disobedient to parents, 31*
*foolish, faithless, heartless, ruthless. 32 Though they know God's righteous*
*decree that those who practice such things deserve to die, they not only do*
*them but give approval to those who practice them.*

*Isaiah 1:2-5, 15-21a, 23*

*2 Hear, O heavens, and give ear, O earth; for the Lord has spoken: "Children*
*have I reared and brought up, but they have rebelled against me. 3 The ox*
*knows its owner, and the donkey its master's crib, but Israel does not know, my*
*people do not understand." 4 Ah, sinful nation, a people laden with iniquity,*
*offspring of evildoers, children who deal corruptly! They have forsaken the*
*Lord, they have despised the Holy One of Israel, they are utterly estranged.*
*5 Why will you still be struck down? Why will you continue to rebel? The whole*
*head is sick, and the whole heart faint. ...15 When you spread out your hands,*
*I will hide my eyes from you; even though you make many prayers, I will not*
*listen; your hands are full of blood. 16 Wash yourselves; make yourselves*
*clean; remove the evil of your deeds from before my eyes; cease to do evil,*
*17 learn to do good; seek justice, correct oppression; bring justice to the*
*fatherless, plead the widow's cause. 18 "Come now, let us reason together,*
*says the Lord: though your sins are like scarlet, they shall be as white as snow;*
*though they are red like crimson, they shall become like wool. 19 If you are*
*willing and obedient, you shall eat the good of the land; 20 but if you refuse*
*and rebel, you shall be eaten by the sword; for the mouth of the Lord has*
*spoken." 21a How the faithful city has become a whore, [become unchaste] she*
*who was full of justice!... 23 Your princes are rebels and companions of*

*thieves. Everyone loves a bribe and runs after gifts. They do not bring justice to the fatherless, and the widow's cause does not come to them.*

*Luke 13:34*
*O Jerusalem, Jerusalem, the city that kills the prophets and stones those who are sent to it! How often would I have gathered your children together as a hen gathers her brood under her wings, and you were not willing!*

****************

Unfortunately, people from all walks of life have been learning to apply what zoologists call the Landscape of Fear. In it, the hazards of proximity to roaring lions sends others into hiding. Then, just like in the animal kingdom, the intimidating lions become kings and rule the territory.

If you turn on a TV, watch video clips on the internet or read news of any kind – it would seem that ours is a nation of people in chaos living according to their own understanding and way of thinking. Threat and Intimidation, though often extremely subtle, are in operation everywhere. Acting in Judgement and Condemnation, we justify our actions on the basis of theirs. The Division between us has reached an all-time high. The worst of our political leaders are majoring in Manipulation using Divisiveness. Divide and conquer - that we might join *them* in *their* purpose. They make people pick sides, Threaten them so that they choose theirs, and then Shame them if they disagree with them.

*Proverbs 3:3-8*
*3 My son, do not forget my teaching, but let your heart keep my commandments, 2 for length of days and years of life and peace they will add to you. 3 Let not steadfast love and faithfulness forsake you; bind them around your neck; write them on the tablet of your heart. 4 So you will find favor and good success in the sight of God and man. 5 Trust in the Lord with all your heart, and do not lean on your own understanding (mind). 6 In all your ways acknowledge him, and he will make straight your paths. 7 Be not wise in your own eyes (mind); fear the Lord, and turn away from evil. 8 It will be healing to your flesh and refreshment to your bones.*

*Galatians 5:17-24*
*17 For the desires of the flesh are against the Spirit, and the desires of the Spirit are against the flesh, for these are opposed to each other, to keep you*

*from doing the things you want to do. 18 But if you are led by the Spirit, you are not under the law. 19 Now the works of the flesh are evident: sexual immorality, impurity, sensuality, 20 idolatry, sorcery, enmity, strife, jealousy, fits of anger, rivalries, dissensions, divisions, 21 envy, drunkenness, orgies, and things like these. I warn you, as I warned you before, that <u>those who (continue to) do such things will not inherit the kingdom of God</u>. 22 But the fruit of the Spirit is love, joy, peace, patience, kindness, goodness, faithfulness, 23 gentleness, self-control; against such things there is no law. 24 And those who belong to Christ Jesus have crucified the flesh with its passions and desires.*

Colossians 3:5-17

*5 Put to death therefore what is earthly in you: sexual immorality, impurity, passion, evil desire, and covetousness, which is idolatry. 6 On account of these the wrath of God is coming. 7 In these you too once walked, when you were living in them. 8 But now you must put them all away: anger, wrath, malice, slander, and obscene talk from your mouth. 9 Do not lie to one another, seeing that you have put off the old self with its practices 10 and have put on the new self, which is being renewed in knowledge after the image of its creator. 11 Here there is not Greek and Jew, circumcised and uncircumcised, barbarian, Scythian, slave, free; but Christ is all, and in all. 12 Put on then, as God's chosen ones, holy and beloved, compassionate hearts, kindness, humility, meekness, and patience, 13 bearing with one another and, if one has a complaint against another, forgiving each other; as the Lord has forgiven you, so you also must forgive. 14 And above all these put on love, which binds everything together in perfect harmony. 15 And let the peace of Christ rule in your hearts, to which indeed you were called in one body. And be thankful. 16 Let the word of Christ dwell in you richly, teaching and admonishing one another in all wisdom, singing psalms and hymns and spiritual songs, with thankfulness in your hearts to God. 17 And whatever you do, in word or deed, do everything in the name of the Lord Jesus, giving thanks to God the Father through him.*

Ephesians 6:10, 11-18

*10 Finally, be strong in the Lord and in the strength of his might. 11 Put on the whole armor of God, that you may be able to stand against the schemes of the devil. 13 Therefore take up the whole armor of God, that you may be able to withstand in the evil day, and having done all, to stand firm. 14 Stand therefore, having fastened on the belt of truth, and having put on the breastplate of righteousness, 15 and, as shoes for your feet, having put on the readiness given by the gospel of peace. 16 In all circumstances take up the shield of faith, with which you can extinguish all the flaming darts of the evil one; 17 and take the helmet of salvation, and the sword of the Spirit, which is the word of God, 18 praying at all times in the Spirit, with all prayer and supplication. To that end, keep alert with all perseverance, making supplication for all the saints.*

****************

So be wise. Paraphrasing Jonathan Cahn's posting from May 12, 2026:

*"What do they need?" "What will be in THEIR best interest?" James 2:8 says, "Love your neighbor as yourself." It's called the Royal Law because it's God's law that He Himself followed. The gospel is God manifesting the Royal Law. He looked at us with love and said, "If I were them, what would I need?" God was your neighbor in the universe and He loved you with all His life, heart and soul. He gave Himself for you. He put Himself in your shoes. He loved you as Himself. It's the Royal Law of the King of the universe. Live by it. As He did for you, you do for others. He loved you; you love them. He put Himself in your place; you put yourself in their place. He lowered Himself to raise you up; you lower yourself to raise them up.*

*Asking Him for His heart of Wisdom, ask of Him, "What would I need if I were them?" Then give "what He says" to them with all your heart, because it will have been balanced by the Mind of Christ, and it will be the will of the Father... because OUR minds alone lack His Wisdom.*

*Those who live by the Royal Law of the King of the universe will be blessed by the King. And their lives, their souls, their heart, their journey, everything in their life, everything in your life, will become royal.*

# *Chapter Six*

## Nothing New Under The Sun

*Ecclesiastes 1:9*
*What has been is what will be, and what has been done is what will be done, and there is nothing new under the sun.*

During the Greek occupation of Israel from 300BC to 150 BC, the relatively new Sadducee sect adopted the culture of their Greek occupiers, merging with them so as to gain governing support over the Jews.

Then, around 200BC, to counter the Sadducees growing departure from Judaism, the Pharisees birthed a new sect. In it, they initiated a distinct and *opposing* religious movement that did not embrace Greek culture but denounced it.

The Pharisees and Sadducees were much like the Democrats and Republicans of our day, each opposing the other, seeking to gain and hold political power over the people. Each sect pressured the people for *what* they needed to know to decide *which side* they should be on. Like our Christian denominations of today, they were arguing about *who* was *right*; and *who* knew *best* how to live a life pleasing to God according to *them. They* debated what *they* thought was necessary to *know*... and therefore what *they* thought the people should be doing.

*Debates are about winners and losers,*
*not Unity and the collective wisdom God provides us together.*

Much like the Democrats and Republicans of today, each slandered the other in Israel's governing body (much like our Congress) called the Sanhedrin. The Sanhedrin was composed of Pharisees, Sadducees, scribes and elders. These are the Jewish politicians who later conjured up the accusations against Jesus that he be put to death.

In 150-100BC, God responded by initiating the Rabbinic/Talmidic way in the small area of Bethsaida, Korazin, and Capernaum on the northern end of the Sea of Galilee. The Rabbinic/Talmidic way didn't exist anywhere else in

Israel at that time. It is also at this time that children began to learn to read and write by memorizing and copying the torah. All of this was to prepare the people of these small towns for Jesus' teaching later upon his arrival.

Then came Rabbi Jesus to oppose the politically Religious and the Religiously political. As a rabbi, He taught, trained, *simplified* and lived out *how to live a life pleasing to God...* contrary to the *what to know and what to do* of the Pharisees and Sadducees.

Jesus continually pointed to the criticality of a personal relationship with God the Father: our hearts after his in a desire to know and accomplish his will. In Conversational Learning, he explained how all scripture pointed to *how to live a life pleasing to God, in right relationship with God*. He spoke of it in the Conversational Learning style of the synagogues of that day; in Conversational Rabbinic/Talmidic Learning with the twelve; in the synagogues on the sabbath; and by piquing the people's interest through his preaching in public - that they might want to know more and more - and be drawn in to Conversational Learning themselves.

Jesus did not have anything good to say about the Pharisees and Sadducees - and now here *we* are *again* - being pressured by the various religions of our day. Much like the Pharisee and Sadducee sects of that day, our 250 Christian denominations are telling us that we would all be better off if we would just follow *them*. King Solomon famously said, "What has been is what will be, and what has been done is what will be done, and there is nothing new under the sun." This has been repeated over and over forever since with the oft quoted words: Those who do not learn from history are condemned to repeat it.

Now, like the Old Testament people of *that* day, most Politics and Religions are using our bibles against us to try to influence us for political power - for the ability to Control us, and so Direct our country's future. Unfortunately, too many of our well-intentioned pastors have become pawns in the game.

As we strive to love, I believe that we should resist the urge to take a political side. As Christ Followers, we do not follow in the things of mankind, we follow Christ our Head, our King, the Reconciler. It's not about who's right and who's wrong, but what is "Love" and what is "Not Love".

Democrats and Republicans have opinions that they are entitled to have, but neither can be totally "right" according to their "Party Platform". Without joining a centrist Independent Party, we must remain independent and vote according to the leading of God. If enough of us do it, they just might move in our direction, that is, God's direction for behavior, and the world will be a better place. If we align with a Party, we are part of the Division. Love is not divisive, Not Love is.

If you feel God leading you into politics, you must certainly go. However, the wiles of the party will surely be working to trick you into becoming one of them. We very much need competent capable and mature Christ Followers to change the divisive discourse. Many are they who have entered in hoping to bring Unity, only to find themselves among the Dividers not all that much later. Be not Deceived!

*1 Corinthians 15:33*
*Do not be deceived: "Bad company ruins good morals."*

It is clear that many, including a portion who call themselves Christian, are finding the Landscape of Fear a very effective tool. The *Life* portion of *Life, Love and Leading* provides a clear scriptural understanding that we are not to be doing what so many of us are doing. *Life* describes what it looks like to communicate in the attitudes of the Beatitudes, Jesus' attitudes, with fruit of the Spirit language and actions, to strengthen relationships and bring better decision making.

When we are mature, balanced and United with him in our hearts, souls and minds, we may more effectively communicate with the lions of this world. Practice utilizing *fruit of the Spirit* language and actions that you more and more *become* a talmid of Jesus, and therefore a more effective communicator doing the will of the Father. Monitor your words and deeds that they be done Kindly, Gently, Perseveringly, Peaceably and with Goodness. As we learn to live with hearts after the Father and in the attitudes of Jesus (Matthew 5:2-12), this posture and humility will prepare us for fruit of the Spirit (Galatians 5:22-23) language and actions in each and every interaction:

*Galatians 5:22-24*
*22 But the fruit of the Spirit is love, joy, peace, patience, kindness, goodness, faithfulness, 23 gentleness, self-control; against such things there is no law. 24 And those who belong to Christ Jesus have crucified the flesh with its passions and desires.*

*Matthew 5:2-12*

*2 And he opened his mouth and taught them, saying: 3 "Blessed are the poor in*
*spirit, for theirs is the kingdom of heaven. 4 "Blessed are those who mourn, for*
*they shall be comforted. 5 "Blessed are the meek, for they shall inherit the*
*earth. 6 "Blessed are those who hunger and thirst for righteousness, for they*
*shall be satisfied. 7 "Blessed are the merciful, for they shall receive mercy.*
*8 "Blessed are the pure in heart, for they shall see God. 9 "Blessed are the*
*peacemakers, for they shall be called sons of God. 10 "Blessed are those who*
*are persecuted for righteousness' sake, for theirs is the kingdom of heaven.*
*11 "Blessed are you when others revile you and persecute you and utter all*
*kinds of evil against you falsely on my account. 12 Rejoice and be glad, for*
*your reward is great in heaven, for so they persecuted the prophets*
*who were before you.*

---

Sadly, these attitudes and behaviors are increasingly rare in our world. Truly, the sins of the parents have been being passed down to the children and their children's children for generations - and look where it has gotten us! Our Father has revealed it to you. How did it happen? Who will reverse the trend? It is so costly! The future of our children is at stake!

*Exodus 20:5-6*

*You shall not worship them or serve them; for I, the Lord your God, am a jealous God, visiting the iniquity of the fathers on the children, on the third and the fourth generations of those who hate Me, but showing loving kindness to thousands, to those who love Me and keep My commandments.*

*Numbers 14:18*

*'The Lord is slow to anger and abundant in loving kindness, forgiving iniquity and transgression; but He will by no means clear the guilty, visiting the iniquity of the fathers on the children to the third and the fourth generations.'*

*Isaiah 65:6-7*

*Behold, it is written before me: "I will not keep silent, but I will repay; I will*
*indeed repay into their lap 7 both your iniquities and your fathers' iniquities*
*together, says the LORD; because they made offerings on the mountains and*
*insulted me on the hills, I will measure into their lap payment*

*for their former deeds."*

*Jeremiah 32:18-19*

*18 You show steadfast love to thousands, but you repay the guilt of fathers to their children after them, O great and mighty God, whose name is the Lord of hosts, 19 great in counsel and mighty in deed, whose eyes are open to all the ways of the children of man, rewarding each one according to his ways and according to the fruit of his deeds.*

*Nahum 1:3a*

*The Lord is slow to anger and great in power,*
*and the Lord will by no means clear the guilty.*

*Ephesians 6:12*

*... we do not wrestle against flesh and blood (people), but against the rulers, against the authorities, against the cosmic powers over this present darkness, against the spiritual forces of evil in the heavenly places.*

*Colossians 2:8*

*See to it that no one takes you captive by philosophy and empty deceit, according to human tradition (use of Authority), according to the elemental spirits of the world, and not according to Christ.*

Culture and traditions are born of the passing down of understandings and misunderstandings that survive. Good ones *and* bad ones. The sins of the parents are passed down to the 3rd and 4th generation. So, too, have both the wisdom and the errors of church leaders been passed down to the 3rd and 4th generation. For generations. For generations of generations.

The best of intentions may lead to the engraining of misunderstandings over time. Our forefathers bought into tiny Deceptions that have grown over the centuries to encompass large swaths of badly mistaken good intentions.

Over the generations, our parents' misunderstandings have then been passed along to cause additional lacks of understanding in their children. Not understanding the ways of God leads to disunity in the family unit and has therefore led to disunity in our nation.

God's Enemies have been planting ever so subtle Deceptions into a portion of the leaders of our seminaries, bible colleges, churches and therefore into our parents and children's children for many hundreds of years. As was described in *Life*, seemingly harmless well-intentioned statements and half-told-truths have been passed down through the ages and continue to be told today. These statements and half-told-truths may sound right to us, but they mislead and confuse the less knowledgeable among us who are still trying to understand who God is. The less knowledgeable then pass them along as *Gospel truths*, when in fact they are not. God births good people, but the Enemy corrupts a portion:

*Matthew 13:24-30*

*24 He put another parable before them, saying, "The kingdom of heaven may be compared to a man who sowed good seed in his field, 25 but while his men were sleeping, his enemy came and sowed weeds among the wheat and went away. 26 So when the plants came up and bore grain, then the weeds appeared also. 27 And the servants of the master of the house came and said to him, 'Master, did you not sow good seed in your field? How then does it have weeds?' 28 He said to them, 'An enemy has done this.' So the servants said to him, 'Then do you want us to go and gather them?' 29 But he said, 'No, lest in gathering the weeds you root up the wheat along with them. 30 Let both grow together until the harvest, and at harvest time I will tell the reapers, "Gather the weeds first and bind them in bundles to be burned, but gather the wheat into my barn."'"*

The Enemy has us on the run, but we have nothing to fear. Who will reverse the trend so that each generation instead passes Wisdom down to the 3rd and 4th generation?

*2 Peter 1:3-4 NIV*

*3 His divine power has given us everything we need for a godly life through our knowledge of him who called us by his own glory and goodness. 4 Through these he has given us his very great and precious promises, so that through them you may participate in the divine nature, having escaped the corruption in the world caused by evil desires.*

*Matthew 5:13-16*

*13 "You are the salt of the earth, but if salt has lost its taste, how shall its saltiness be restored? It is no longer good for anything except to be thrown out and trampled under people's feet. 14 "You are the light of the world. A city set on a hill cannot be hidden. 15 Nor do people light a lamp and put it under a basket, but on a stand, and it gives light to all in the house. 16 In the same way, let your light shine before others, so that they may see your good works and give glory to your Father who is in heaven.*

---

*O Adonai:*
*Sprinkle us like salt across our communities, each grain reflecting your light, that by your words and actions through us, as we participate with you, we illuminate their path home. That none should perish, but live eternally in the joy of relationship with you.*

*1 John 2:3-6*
*3 And by this we know that we have come to know him, if we keep his commandments. 4 Whoever says "I know him" but does not keep his commandments is a liar, and the truth is not in him, 5 but whoever keeps his word, in him truly the love of God is perfected. By this we may know that we are in him: 6 whoever says he abides in him ought to walk in the same way in which he walked.*

*1 John 2:28*
*And now, little children, abide in him, so that when he appears we may have confidence and not shrink from him in shame at his coming.*

*John 10:27*
*My sheep hear my voice, and I know them, and they follow me.*

*Matthew 18:3*
*"Truly, I say to you, unless you turn and become like children, you will never enter the kingdom of heaven.*

---

# Chapter Seven

## Let Us Make Man As Our Imager

If you want to learn to love well in this brief life, take it to the Father. Learn it from the Son. Be led by our Helper and Encourager, the Holy Spirit. You are a unique individual, only God knows you well enough to help you fully.

Who is he? He is the Father, the Director of all things. Even Jesus submits to him and is obedient to his will and timing. His ways are not our ways. He knows the plans he has for us. He is doing his works in us, for us.

Who is he? He is the Son, Jesus the Christ, the great Reconciler. He came that we might be reconciled with the Father and with each other. He has been given authority to rule over the earth *with* the Father. He said, *"Here I am - it is written about me in the scroll - I have come to do your will, O God."* He is the King of Kings and Lord of Lords.

Who is he? He is the Holy Spirit, the Active Implementer of God's will. He leads us to serve in ways that are uniquely our own. After his resurrection, Jesus told us that he would send his Holy Spirit to dwell within us and compel us to do all that he has taught us. He admonished his *talmidim* to not do *anything* until the Holy Spirit showed up.

Made in his image (biblical language scholars prefer "as his imager" – as imagers reflecting his glory) and baptized into his family, you have been given the power of his Presence for *becoming*, so that you may operate in the character and attributes of the great Director, Reconciler and Active Implementer.

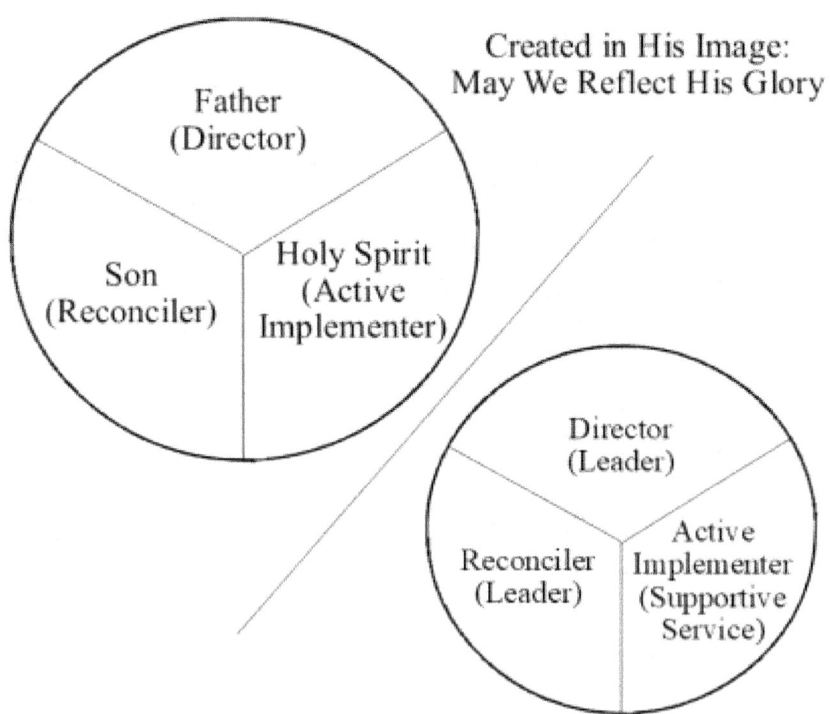


Who are you? As his imager reflecting his image, your Father characteristics come into play whenever you have directional leadership responsibility. Your characteristics of the Son come into play anytime you step in to offer a path to reconciliation between people or between people and God. Your Holy Spirit characteristics come into play when you actively serve to implement the will of God on earth as it is in heaven. As an imager of the Godhead, you are one person with three distinct roles that may be developed to more and more reflect those of Adonai (our triune God).

We are not perfect, but we have been given a great gift. He who *is* perfect has placed us on earth to model our behavior after him who created us and in contrast to the Powers of Darkness that tell us to do otherwise. In relationship with him and made as imagers, we were made to reflect his glory.

*With whom do you have directional leadership responsibility? Your family? Your employees? With whomever it is, use that responsibility in the character and Unity of the great Director, our Father in heaven. Where there is conflict, offer reconciliation in the character and Unity of the great Reconciler, the Son of the living God, King of Kings and Lord of Lords. Where there is need, serve in Unity where he uniquely inspires you, with the help of the Holy Spirit and in the unique giftedness he has provided for that purpose.*

Depending upon the setting, we are sometimes Directors, sometimes Reconcilers and sometimes Active Implementers – but we tend to be more frequently one of them than we are the other two. Some of us are more gifted for strategic direction, vision, planning and in leading productivity. Others are more gifted for the strategic planning necessary to lead and maintain relational Unity. And still others prefer to spend most of their time in Support of the leadership of Directors and Reconcilers.

Herein lies our difficulty: Directors and Reconcilers both have leader roles.

*The Father (the Director of all things) and the Son (the King of Kings and Lord of Lords) both have a leadership focus that is perfectly balanced in strategy, planning and purpose. The Son leads with the Father. We tend toward the use of Individuated Authoritarian Leadership and Leverage in order to gain or sustain Control - and thereby lose the Co-Leadership synergy that Adonai models for us in Unity.*

As described in depth in *Life*, when we lead individually with an Authority bias, we fall short due to the blind spots generated by the overuse of our strengths and in avoidance of our areas of weakness. We need each other to apply the broad strength of our *collective* giftedness. All the information from these brings more balance to our collective discernment of the will of the Father, the mind of Christ, the leading of the Spirit and therefore *Unity* in our *collective decision making*.

People with a Director focus are not as relational as people with a Reconciler focus. Unaware, or more likely misunderstood, teams of Directors and Reconcilers tend to find disagreement as one tries to speed along efficiently and productively while the other sees a need to talk it through to be sure that there will not be relational damage. If the Director is the boss – relationships suffer. If the Reconciler is the boss – productivity suffers. In truth, as described in great depth and detail in *Life*, none of us are to be the boss. No one is to be in authority except Christ who is the head of all things. We are just body parts who are to be collectively doing the will of the Father as One, as Jesus described in John 17.

Collectively led by the power of the Holy Spirit, taught and trained by Jesus, with the Father in us doing his works – each portion of the Body of Christ does its part. Directors and Reconcilers are simply leaders who are to *collectively* discern the will of the Father in Unity as *Adonai* (our triune God) leads *us*.

*When we use Authority, Unity is not our number one priority.*

****************

What do you do when a friend or associate has a better idea? You follow theirs! Jesus said that he only does and says what the Father tells him. So will we as we learn how his ways are better than our ways. Our hearts, souls and minds will respond, "YOUR will be done, O God, not mine!"

*John 14:21*
*Whoever has my commandments and keeps them, he it is who loves me. And he who loves me will be loved by my Father, and I will love him and manifest myself to him."*

*John 15:9-11*
*9 As the Father has loved me, so have I loved you. Abide in my love. 10 If you keep my commandments, you will abide in my love, just as I have kept my Father's commandments and abide in his love. 11 <u>These things I have spoken to you, that my joy may be in you, and that your joy may be full</u>.*

*John 5:19*
*So Jesus said to them, "Truly, truly, I say to you, the Son can do <u>nothing of his own accord</u>, but only what he sees the Father doing. For <u>whatever the Father does, that the Son does likewise.</u>*

*John 12:49-50*
*49 For <u>I have not spoken on my own authority</u>, but the Father who sent me has himself given me a commandment - <u>what to say and what to speak</u>. 50 And I know that <u>his commandment is eternal life</u>. <u>What I say, therefore, I say as the Father has told me</u>."*

*Matthew 6:9-10*
*9 Pray then like this: "Our Father in heaven, hallowed be your name. 10 <u>Your</u> kingdom come, <u>your</u> will be done...*

It would not be fair for him to tell us to do his will for the coming of his kingdom and then not give us a way of knowing what it is. We know his will because he tells us! As we mature in Christ, what we were in the natural will be overcome by the spiritual and bring us more into his likeness - and our eyes and ears will become more and more attuned to hearing and seeing his will as we do. Otherwise…

*Matthew 13:14-15*

*14 Indeed, in their case the prophecy of Isaiah is fulfilled that says: “‘“You will indeed hear but never understand, and you will indeed see but never perceive.” 15 For this people's heart has grown dull, and with their ears they can barely hear, and their eyes they have closed, lest they should see with their eyes and hear with their ears and understand with their heart and turn, and I would heal them.’*

Our Adversary is so deceptive. Once we believe that we may take Authority over others, we will then begin to use *manipulate to control* strategies as Leverage to make people do what we want. Therefore: *“You will indeed hear but never understand, and you will indeed see but never perceive.”*

But these are not God’s ways. One with him, we instead humbly share information in fruit of the Spirit language (Galatians 5:22-23) and in the attitudes of Jesus (Matthew 5:2-12) offering fruit of the Spirit – to strengthen relationships. In this way we will grow in discipline, and therefore in our ability to hear, understand, see and perceive:

*2 Corinthians 3:16-18*

*16 But when one turns to the Lord, the veil is removed. 17 Now the Lord is the Spirit, and where the Spirit of the Lord is, there is freedom. 18 And we all, with unveiled face, beholding the glory of the Lord, are being transformed into the same image from one degree of glory to another.*
*For this comes from the Lord who is the Spirit.*

*2 Thessalonians 3:3*

*… the Lord is faithful. He will establish you*
*and guard you against the evil one.*

*Philippians 2:13*

*for it is God who works in you, both to will and to work*

*for his good pleasure.*

*Philippians 1:6*
*And I am sure of this, that he who began a good work in you will bring it to completion at the day of Jesus Christ.*

*1 Thessalonians 5:23-24*
*23 <u>Now may the God of peace himself sanctify you completely</u>, and may your whole spirit and soul and body be kept blameless at the coming of our Lord Jesus Christ. 24 <u>He who calls you is faithful; he will surely do it</u>.*

*2 Thessalonians 1:11-12*
*11 To this end we always pray for you, that our God may make you worthy of his calling and may <u>fulfill every resolve for good and every work of faith by his power</u>, 12 so that the name of our Lord Jesus may be glorified in you, and you in him, according to the grace of our God and the Lord Jesus Christ.*

*Hebrews 10:35-36*
*35 Therefore <u>do not throw away your confidence, which has a great reward</u>. 36 For <u>you have need of endurance</u>, so that when <u>you have done the will of God</u> you may receive what is promised.*

*Hebrews 13:20-21*
*20 Now may the God of peace who brought again from the dead our Lord Jesus, the great shepherd of the sheep, by the blood of the eternal covenant, 21 equip you with everything good that you may <u>do his will, working in us that which is pleasing in his sight</u>, through Jesus Christ, to whom be glory forever and ever. Amen.*

Sharing information as God does, more and more we will *become* Gentle, Patient, Kind and Persevering in Goodness so that the information we share is *void of Manipulation or Coercion*. As the Holy Spirit helps with Self-Control, we will offer a *desired* outcome in the Hope of growing Peace, Joy and Love. Then, like God, we will remain available for Dialogue and let them choose for themselves.

There is a difference between unconditional love and enablement. Like God, we are to provide the information. Like God, we are to allow others to make their own choice, no matter how foolish – and continue to love them unconditionally. One of the expressions of that love is to allow them to go out and learn on their own what they have chosen not to learn from the Wisdom of God and others. When we love unconditionally, we bathe them in prayer when they go their own way, asking God to intervene that they may learn quickly. Enablement *saves them quickly* such that they learn little and so *continue to* repeat their folly. As we Gently inform with Patience and Kindness, we are not telling them how to behave - we are telling them how God says to behave.

Functioning as a family, business, church, community, nation and world we tend to lose our leadership balance (and therefore Unity) as we scale in size. We need to be very intentional if we will maintain Unity as we achieve scale over time. This requires leaders who are more interested in collectively discerning the will of God for the common good than advancing their own ideas and interests. Later in the *Leading* section, we will see that we have been somewhat effective at it in our communities and in our nation for most of our 200 years, but not so much now.

*When Authority is allowed to develop, speaking freely will eventually be associated with risk, and squelch the sharing of Wisdom. However, when we instead honor and value the collective wisdom, all may speak up safely. When all are committed to the sharing of the collective wisdom, our only risk is in not using fruit of the Spirit language in the attitudes of Jesus. Fruit of the Spirit language with the proper attitude facilitates Unity, even while iron sharpens iron.*

*When we use Authority, Unity is not our number one priority.*

# Chapter Eight

## Willing Participants In Creative Collaboration

His primary desire is a Love relationship *with* us, our hearts after his, us finding Joy together as we do *his* will, as we make Connections with others that more and more grow us in Love *with* him *and* others – that none should perish. He is offering us a chance to Accept him and his will, to accomplish that which he has for us. *To participate with him in causing that which has not yet been fully caused, in releasing that which has not yet been fully released and/or fulfilling that which has not yet been fulfilled.*

*John 14:12*
*"Truly, truly, I say to you, whoever believes in me will also do the works that I do; and greater works than these will he do,*
*because I am going to the Father.*

*Philippians 1:6*
*And I am sure of this, that he who began a good work in you*
*will bring it to completion at the day of Jesus Christ.*

*1 Corinthians 6:19*
*Or do you not know that your body is a temple of the Holy Spirit within you, whom you have from God? You are not your own,*

When we think of ourselves as mobile temples in which he lives, as houses of prayer committed to knowing him, knowing his ways and knowing his will, we will find ourselves praying unceasingly. That is, in the Hebrew, in *continual conversational worship.*

*1 Thessalonians 5:17-18*
*17 pray (inquire, ask, petition, request) without ceasing, 18 give thanks in all circumstances; for this is the will of God in Christ Jesus for you.*

Gaining this conversational intimacy, this all-day-long attentiveness, this ability to wear an earbud and microphone so to speak as we go through our day, requires a process. Cultivating an ear that hears God requires education, training and discernment to know when it is his Spirit speaking to our spirit and when it is a Rejector spirit attempting to Deceive.

For me, it was helpful to transition into an all-day conversation by recognizing that he is truly watching our every move and is hopeful to talk with us about whatever we are doing or contemplating. For those who think of him like a penitent, punishing boss complaining about our every mistake, this would be counterproductive. But for those of us who will see him as he really is - an encouraging life coach cheering us on to success after success, little by little, bit by bit, more and more and glory by glory; conformed to the image of his Son (2 Corinthians 3:18 and Romans 8:29) - we will find ourselves learning to talk with others the way he talks with us: truthfully, humbly and in fruit of the Spirit language. Failing him less and less.

Sharing information as God does, we will be Gentle, Patient, Kind and Persevering in Goodness so that the information we share is void of Manipulation or Coercion. As the Holy Spirit helps us in Self-Control, we will offer a desired outcome to grow Peace, Joy and Love. Then, like God, we will remain available for Dialogue and let them choose for themselves.

He calls us friend and walks with us as we walk with him, giving us Peace that surpasses understanding throughout all our days – no matter what trouble the world throws at us. *Becoming* more like him, we will truly walk in an attitude of gratitude that others will notice and appreciate - especially through adversity.

*John 15:15*

*No longer do I call you servants, for the servant does not know what his master is doing; but I have called you friends, for all that I have heard from my Father I have made known to you.*

*Proverbs 17:17*

*A friend loves at all times, and a brother is born for adversity.*

*Philippians 4:6-8*

*6 do not be anxious about anything, but in everything by prayer and supplication with thanksgiving let your requests be made known to God. 7 And the peace of God, which surpasses all understanding, will guard your hearts and your minds in Christ Jesus. 8 Finally, brothers, whatever is true, whatever* *is honorable, whatever is just, whatever is pure, whatever is lovely, whatever is commendable, if there is any excellence, if there is anything worthy of praise, <u>think about these things</u>.*

He is simply saying, "I am here. Talk to me. *Listen* for me and listen *to* me. You can trust me. I'll prove it to you. I will help you learn my ways; I will Direct you, and you will succeed more and more in reflecting my Love to those around you."

*Father, thank you that we may be creative in our relationship with you. Thank you that you actually desire our collaboration! Thank you that we may talk over possible solutions with you and ask you to lead us to understand which will be best. May we always agree with you for your will, even if it be difficult! May we always notice the moments when anxiety is trying to creep in, and maintain your Peace. Help us that we not give in to Fear and enter into temptation. Deliver us from evil! Your kingdom come, your will be done, thank you that you will help me see the difference between yours and mine. Teach me and train me that, more and more, I walk in your ways and accomplish your will.*

Children follow their parents as they help them mature into adulthood. Away from selfishness. Away from impetuous actions. Away from destructive passions. As we mature into adulthood, we do and say according to the will of our Father in heaven more and more.

*Matthew 18:1-2*

*2 And calling to him a child, he put him in the midst of them 3 and said, "<u>Truly, I say to you, unless you turn and become like children, you will never enter the kingdom of heaven.</u>*

*Colossians 3:5a, 7-9*

*5 Put to death therefore what is earthly in you… 7 In these you too once walked, when you were living in them. 8 But now you must put them all away: anger, wrath, malice, slander, and obscene talk from your mouth. 9 Do not lie to one another, seeing that you have put off the old self with its practices*

*Proverbs 6:16-19*

*16 There are six things that the Lord hates, seven that are an abomination to him: 17 haughty eyes, a lying tongue, and hands that shed innocent blood, 18 a heart that devises wicked plans, feet that make haste to run to evil, 19 a false witness who breathes out lies, and One who sows discord among brothers.*

*Ephesians 4:29-32*

*29 Let no corrupting talk come out of your mouths, but only such as is good for building up, as fits the occasion, that it may give grace to those who hear.*
*30 And do not grieve the Holy Spirit of God, by whom you were sealed for the day of redemption. 31 Let all bitterness and wrath and anger and clamor and slander be put away from you, along with all malice. 32 Be kind to one another, tenderhearted, forgiving one another, as God in Christ forgave you.*

*Colossians 3:12-15*

*12 Put on then, as God's chosen ones, holy and beloved, compassionate hearts, kindness, humility, meekness, and patience, 13 bearing with one another and, if one has a complaint against another, forgiving each other; as the Lord has forgiven you, so you also must forgive. 14 And above all these put on love, which binds everything together in perfect harmony. 15 And let the peace of Christ rule in your hearts, to which indeed you were called in one body. And be thankful.*

As we mature in Christ, what we were in the natural will be overcome by his Spirit and bring us more into his likeness - and our eyes and ears will become more and more attuned to hearing and seeing his will as we do (2 Corinthians 3:18 and Romans 8:29: little by little, success by success, glory by glory; conformed to the image of his Son). Otherwise:

*Matthew 13:15*

*For this people's heart has grown dull, and with their ears they can barely hear, and their eyes they have closed, lest they should see with their eyes and hear with their ears and understand with their heart and turn, and I would heal them.'*

*Romans 1:28-32*

*28 And since they did not see fit to acknowledge God, God gave them up to a debased mind to do what ought not to be done. 29 They were filled with all manner of unrighteousness, evil, covetousness, malice. They are full of envy, murder, strife, deceit, maliciousness. They are gossips, 30 slanderers, haters of God, insolent, haughty, boastful, inventors of evil, disobedient to parents, 31 foolish, faithless, heartless, ruthless. 32 Though they know God's righteous decree that those who practice such things deserve to die, they not only do them but give approval to those who practice them.*

Why are we falling for the destructive *manipulative deception* of our people and politicians? The only evidence we need to withstand them is recognition that their fruit cannot be of God. They are about *Enmity, Strife, Jealousy, Fits of Anger, Rivalries, Dissensions, Divisions, ... and things like these*. His never is.

God will not produce bad fruit. "Not fruit of the Spirit" is "not God". God's purpose humbly brings forward information, facilitates thoughtful discussion and promotes United action.

*Proverbs 27:17*
*Iron sharpens iron, and one man sharpens another.*

Still, how we say what we say is just as important as our position on it. Iron sharpening iron through fruit of the Spirit language in conversations aimed at discerning the will of God (not ours) brings greater Unity, synergy and therefore productivity. The Fear Mongerer Slanders their opponent, Shaming them for their position and Accuses them of all of the things that they themselves are doing. If it is not facilitating Unity but uses any one of a number of *manipulative methods* to Divide and Conquer so as to Control outcomes, it is "not God". "Not love" is simply "not God".

*"Gossip can do its work with tones of voice or a roll of the eye. While we may think of gossip as a harmless diversion, the New Testament lists it along with envy, murder, strife, and hating God" (Romans 1:8-30). Timothy and Kathy Keller, "The Songs of Jesus," Viking, 2015, p. 86*

Leaning on our own understanding, we have *become* a Hard-Hearted nation in Chaos, *trusting ourselves* to figure out what we should do. We think our way through - rationalizing our behavior with hearts as cold as ice. Justifying our actions based upon theirs. Rather, if we will *trust him* for his solution, we will see that his answer has been before us all along:

*Go, make talmidim of all nations...*

Unfortunately, so many of us have been focusing upon baptizing and been neglecting the making of talmidim who desire to *become just like* their rabbi Jesus. We have watered down the foundational aspects of who God is and what he desires of us such that our children hardly know him, our families are *becoming* weaker, and the Division and Degradation of our nation is on the increase. Though it takes longer and requires one-on-one *life on life* effort - we need to return to the making of *talmidim* if we will ever reverse the trend.

Pew Research and Barna Group studies have found that there is very little difference between the lifestyles & behaviors of people who call themselves Christian and those who do not. Things are getting worse:

- In 1971, 90% identified as Christian. In 2008: 77%. In 2019: 65%.
- In 1999, 73% were members of a church. In 2019 that number was 47%.

*Much of what many of our present day pastor/teachers do explains scripture so as to provide us head knowledge for life application. This is the individualistic Hellenistic approach of life application via increasing knowledge, not the talmidic approach for becoming just like our rabbi Jesus. This may be the biggest reason that the church in the USA has been in decline for so very many decades. It is an indictment of the ways of our seminaries, bible colleges, pastors, teachers and parenting down through the generations that these numbers have fallen off so dramatically.*

*Let us endeavor to offer the talmidic approach,*
*that we might grow hearts after our Father.*

We must now, more and more, offer ourselves up as a work in process to the Father, Son and Holy Spirit - *with unveiled face, beholding the glory of the Lord, and be transformed into the same image from one degree of glory to another* (2 Corinthians 3:18). That we make *talmidim*, doing the will of the Father.

Trust him. Do not be concerned, like many are, that your bible knowledge and understanding are insufficient. If *your* heart is after *his*, you are ready for whomever *he* will give you on any given day. As you go through your day, just ask him to give you a nudge for those who *are* yours to engage as well as identify those with whom you *are not* to engage. He will be faithful to train you as you go, little by little, bit by bit, success by success! Go and make talmidim!

*Father, precious is your Presence. Your kingdom come. Yes, Lord, bring it. Manifest it, establish it, make it as real on the whole earth as it is in heaven. We agree with you and submit to you for the expansion of your kingdom, not ours. Your will be done, because ours is inferior to yours and yours is best for all – best on earth as it is best in heaven. May the whole world be fed today, with both physical and spiritual food, and forgive as you forgive. May we not enter into temptation, deliver us from Evil! Give us justice against our Adversaries, O God! May they repent, turn to you, be healed, and follow you all of the days of their lives. Send laborers, O God, and lead us to succeed in being ones ourselves!*

Such a brief and simple prayer. Yet it encompasses the whole world!

# Chapter Nine

## Before The Birth Of The Christ

As you may recall from chapter 33 of *Life*, around 150-100 BC God started a new discipleship track in Bethsaida, Korazin and Capernaum for the coming of the Messiah. As you may also recall, the role of the rabbi was to "teach the people *how* to live a life pleasing to God. As you also know from *Life*, talmidim are what we in the USA erroneously call disciples, students and apprentices. The goal of Jesus' talmidim was to *become just like him*. And that this is what he wants of us.

*It is more than the practical application of the knowledge gained. It is more than taking actions based upon our understanding of his teachings. A talmid of Rabbi Jesus will have a heart after the Father, be growing to reflect the very character of Jesus and be gaining the mind and attitudes of Christ.*

The focus of a follower of Jesus is not just to know what Jesus taught, but to *be* what Jesus *was*. Spending every minute of every day in *continual conversational worship* with God the Father, Son and Holy Spirit, we will *more and more* know what to do or say in any situation. When we gather together, we may also expect that Adonai will *lead us together* as we identify the *collective wisdom* he is giving to each of us as Body Parts in our *personal* continual conversational worship. Just as he did in the synagogues of Bethsaida, Korazin and Capernaum during Jesus' day.

*On the sabbath, all of the rabbis from the insulas of the town (often five or more rabbis with hundreds of people in attendance) would gather in the synagogue to conversationally consider the appointed text of that sabbath day. There would be a reading or two from the Torah and/or Tanakh, and the reader could share a brief testimony regarding the scripture selections for the day. Then the people would listen to the rabbis discuss the text so as to enlighten them with their thoughts on the historical context, likely using related text, each including their interpretations - with respectful consideration of differing perspectives a common element.*

With several rabbis present, no one rabbi could steer the people in an unhealthy direction over time. Interestingly, it was culturally acceptable for *anyone* present to add to the discussion, request clarification in a related text, provide a testimony or even disagree with something that had been shared. In this way, the collective wisdom of *all* the people was available for consideration *by all the people*. In this way, faith was made more personal.

In this way, children might hear a testimony from their uncle; or a grandfather their son; and in so doing create the opportunity to discuss it personally together later – expanding upon the learning and adding depth to what was shared.

In *conversational* style, God could send in his *Encouragers*, *Disruptors* or *Correctors* to contribute to the discussions and raise up issues and scripture for community deliberation. It was this setup that made it possible for Jesus (and later the apostle Paul) to speak *in any synagogue on any sabbath*. This is also one of the reasons that young Jesus was able to speak and amaze so many of those present – before he ever started his three-year ministry.

*The lone teacher setup is a heady situation that risks people becoming teacher followers rather than talmidim of Jesus. With several rabbis present, no one rabbi could steer the people in an unhealthy direction over time. In conversational style, God could send in his Encouragers, Disruptors or Correctors to contribute to the discussions and raise up issues and scripture for community deliberation. It was this setup that made it possible for Jesus (and later the apostle Paul) to speak in any synagogue on any sabbath.*

****************

Two thousand years later, we have lost the context of this and many other portions of scripture. Because we are not from that era, we have also lost the images those words would immediately evoke culturally in their listeners.

When Jesus said go and make talmidim of all nations, he did not say go and teach people the Bible so that they could practically apply the information to their lives, he said to go make talmidim!

If *we* will endeavor to *become* just like Jesus, the making of talmidim will require *individual* conversational time in ongoing *life-on-life* discussion. Not forsaking the fellowship, a talmid will also be associated with some sort of *group* of talmidim - continually discussing *how to live the life of a talmid*. Not only that, but *how to help others understand what it means* to live a life pleasing to God as described in the Old and New Testaments.

Though Jesus taught thousands from a boat or a mountainside, the teaching that changed the world started *both as a group and individually* with the twelve. I wonder how many of the twelve were eventually involved in ongoing life-on-life conversations with the 70, and how many of the 70 were involved in life-on-life conversations with the 500? I wonder how often it would happen that an inquiring mind could not ask their question of Jesus because he was so surrounded by others trying to do the same. I wonder how often they would then elect to ask their question of one of his talmidim, thereby initiating a life-on-life opportunity for *them*: "Hey, John, you are one of his guys, what does Jesus say, or maybe, what does Jesus think about this.....?"

What I *do* know, is that Jesus was not involved in ongoing life-on-life conversations with all of the 70 or the 500, there was simply not enough time in the day! Clearly, Jesus' way was to make talmidim who would make talmidim. As an individual Christ Follower, do you have anyone that gets *that* kind of time with *you*?

****************

The Bible was written to the people of *that* day. It was not written *to* us; it was written *to them* and *for us*. We admonish people to read their Bibles each day, and we teach them *what* the Bible says each week in our *tradition of lecture*, but many are having difficulty with understanding the *how*. Like his talmidim, we need to have the *life of the Christ* opened up to us *in context* if we will *comprehend the how* of living the God-led life - with hearts after our Father, eyes that see and ears that hear. Otherwise, without individual conversational time, we are causing them to be always seeing, but never perceiving. (Matthew 13:14, Isaiah 6:9, Mark 4:12)

Like the two who encountered Jesus *conversationally* on the road to Emmaus (Luke 24:13-35), their hearts will burn as the scriptures are opened up to them.

Like the story of Philip and the Eunuch (Acts 8:26-40), people need to have the scriptures opened up to them *conversationally* if they will *comprehend what they are reading.*

Like the story of Priscilla and Aquila pulling Apollos to the side *conversationally* for the deeper understanding (Acts 18:24-28), how will we support the passionate in passing along the *whole* Bible, context and all? Like Apollos, who eventually went to Achaia and powerfully and *conversationally* refuted the Jews in public, will our passionate people be fully prepared to *go*?

Much of what our present-day leaders do on Sundays *preaches* scripture so as to provide us head knowledge for *life application*. This is not the *talmidic* approach for *becoming just like our Rabbi Jesus*, but rather the individualistic Hellenistic *lecture* approach born in the Constantine era and which became common throughout Europe. Now, just like Europe, littered with huge empty cathedrals, have we fallen victim to our lack of understanding of how to *scale* in the family of God? According to ChurchLeadership.org, every year more than 4000 churches close their doors compared to just over 1000 new church starts. On average we are losing a net of eight churches each day!

The church in the USA was birthed by the talmidic families of God who escaped Europe in pursuit of freedom. Unfortunately, more and more have adopted the Constantine *preaching* path and process over the past 100 years. Looking back, this just seemed to make more sense as our communities grew from small towns and villages of people who knew each other, into cities of the faceless and nameless!

*Without conversational worship experiences, how can we expect them to learn how to live a life pleasing to God as a talmid?*

I believe that this *Tradition of Lecture*, was passed down to the 3rd and the 4th generation in the USA from roughly a hundred years ago as our small towns and villages of people who knew each other grew into nameless and faceless cities, and that this is the biggest reason that the church has been in decline for so very many decades. While it is an indictment of the ways of our seminaries, Bible colleges, pastors, teachers and parenting down through the generations that our numbers have fallen off so drastically, the *lecture model* was initially *a logical sounding seed Satan sowed in Deception* that we simply did not understand!

*En masse*, we tend to give people the facts and the logic and fight to persuade them for saving faith and helpful actions. Then, after baptism, continue our fact-filled logical Hellenistic *lecture* approach with weekly self-help Bible teaching and encouragements to serve. As we keep their brains engaged in thinking it all through - *without ongoing conversational opportunities in which to ask their questions, and lost in their heads* - many will walk away. Many *have* walked away, and so our families and nation are falling apart.

We would do well to reconsider our tradition of individuals teaching to gatherings by lecture. Rather, let's afford people conversational iron sharpening iron opportunities as Jesus and the apostles did.

****************

*What if we were to change our approach so as to better facilitate hearts after God with talmidim conversationally? What if we adopted the method the Father prepared in advance for Jesus in the synagogues of The Triangle so that all people may be involved in personal conversational learning each week? What if 12 were sufficiently trained to support the 70 and them the 500?*

What if we were to instead *go* into our communities like Jesus *went,* to pique the curiosity of the people such that some came to our Sunday gatherings for conversational learning? What if the kind of teaching we do now on Sundays (like Jesus did from a boat or mountainside) happened instead in our community centers, our parks, our marketplaces, our homeless encampments and on our street corners? What if denominationally disparate groups of pastor/teachers advertised a day each month where they would take turns using their current Sunday teaching gifts for several hours together in the local community center? What if *our* target audience was as *Jesus'* target audience was - and was supported there by *each of our congregations'* 12, 70 and 500?

What if the assimilated talmidim used these opportunities to invite people to the monthly community gatherings? What if that led people to come to our Sunday gatherings to conversationally learn how to live a life pleasing to God?

What if our marketing simply used the ongoing theme of "How To Live A Life Pleasing To God!"? What if we interspersed two or three of the nearly 100 on-location video teachings of Ray Vander Laan that our people might experience the Bible in its historical context? (That The World May Know ThatTheWorldMayKnow.com)

If you're a megachurch, what if the Sunday gatherings began in the auditorium and then broke out into the smaller rooms where five or six of the 500 could lead conversational discussion with the groups in each room? 500 ÷ 6 = 83 potential rooms where this could happen each week. What if our conversational small group time mid-week was led by *more than one* of the 500 in the Co-Leadership style described in *Leading*?

As is also described in *Leading*, if we will set the ground rules for respectful conversation even the most intense Sunday group discussions with the lost may be kept safe.

# *Chapter Ten*

## Open Up The Scriptures To Me
## Establish In Me Your Will And Your Ways

*1 Thessalonians 5:17-18*
*17 pray (inquire, ask, petition, request) without ceasing, 18 give thanks in all circumstances; for this is the will of God in Christ Jesus for you.*

*Luke 24:13-35*
*13 That very day two of them were going to a village named Emmaus,*
*about seven miles from Jerusalem, 14 and they were talking with each*
*other about all these things that had happened. 15 While they were talking*
*and discussing together, Jesus himself drew near and went with*
*them. 16 But their eyes were kept from recognizing him. 17 And he said to*
*them, "What is this conversation that you are holding with each other as*
*you walk?" And they stood still, looking sad. 18 Then one of them, named*
*Cleopas, answered him, "Are you the only visitor to Jerusalem who does*
*not know the things that have happened there in these days?" 19 And he*
*said to them, "What things?" And they said to him, "Concerning Jesus of*
*Nazareth, a man who was a prophet mighty in deed and word before God*
*and all the people, 20 and how our chief priests and rulers delivered him*
*up to be condemned to death, and crucified him. 21 But we had hoped that*
*he was the one to redeem Israel. Yes, and besides all this, it is now the third*
*day since these things happened. 22 Moreover, some women of our*
*company amazed us. They were at the tomb early in the*
*morning, 23 and when they did not find his body, they came back saying*
*that they had even seen a vision of angels, who said that he was*
*alive. 24 Some of those who were with us went to the tomb and found it just*
*as the women had said, but him they did not see." 25 And he said to*
*them, "O foolish ones, and slow of heart to believe all that the prophets*
*have spoken! 26 Was it not necessary that the Christ should suffer these*
*things and enter into his glory?" 27* ***And beginning with Moses and all the***
***Prophets, he interpreted to them in all the Scriptures the things***
***concerning himself****. 28 So they drew near to the village to which they were*

*going. He acted as if he were going farther, 29 but they urged him strongly, saying, "Stay with us, for it is toward evening and the day is now far spent." So he went in to stay with them. 30 When he was at table with them, he took the bread and blessed and broke it and gave it to them. 31 And their eyes were opened, and they recognized him. And he vanished from their sight. 32 They said to each other,* ***"Did not our hearts burn within us while he talked to us on the road, while he opened to us the Scriptures?"*** *33 And they rose that same hour and returned to Jerusalem. And they found the eleven and those who were with them gathered together, 34 saying, "The Lord has risen indeed, and has appeared to Simon!" 35 Then they told what had happened on the road, and how he was known to them in the breaking of the bread.*

*Luke 24:44-49a*

*44 Then he said to them, "These are my words that I spoke to you while I was still with you, that everything written about me in the Law of Moses and the Prophets and the Psalms must be fulfilled." 45* ***Then he opened their minds to understand the Scriptures****, 46 and said to them, "Thus it is written, that the Christ should suffer and on the third day rise from the dead, 47 and that repentance for the forgiveness of sins should be proclaimed in his name to all nations, beginning from Jerusalem. 48 You are witnesses of these things. 49 And behold, I am sending the promise of my Father upon you.*

*Acts 8:27-35*

*27 And he rose and went. And there was an Ethiopian, a eunuch, a court official of Candace, queen of the Ethiopians, who was in charge of all her treasure. He had come to Jerusalem to worship 28 and was returning, seated in his chariot, and he was reading the prophet Isaiah. 29 And the Spirit said to Philip, "Go over and join this chariot." 30 So Philip ran to him and heard him reading Isaiah the prophet and asked, "Do you understand what you are reading?" 31 And he said, "****How can I, unless someone guides me?****" And he invited Philip to come up and sit with him. 32 Now the passage of the Scripture that he was reading was this:*

*"Like a sheep he was led to the slaughter and like a lamb before its shearer is silent, so he opens not his mouth. 33 In his humiliation justice was denied him. Who can describe his generation? For his life is taken away from the earth."*

*34 And the eunuch said to Philip, "About whom, I ask you, does the prophet say this, about himself or about someone else?" 35* ***Then Philip opened his mouth, and beginning with this Scripture he told him the good news about Jesus.***

*Meet with me and open up the scriptures to me, O God, that your kingdom become visibly manifest in me and that your will be done always and everywhere in my life - all day long every day! Introduce me to those you have prepared for me in advance, that I open up your scriptures to them also.*

*I am confident that you are opening my mind to understand and are Teaching me, O Jesus; That you are Leading me, O Spirit; and are in me Doing Your Works, O Father, that I not enter into temptation but be attentive to you all day long. Deliver me from Evil lest I do what I think and speak my mind!*

*Adonai, thank you that you encourage us with your Presence, moving in our hearts, souls & minds - drawing us closer and closer to yourself, becoming more and more like you. Do your works in us that we not enter into temptation, but be delivered from Evil. We greatly desire to participate with you to establish, strengthen and multiply your people. Give us justice against our Adversaries, O God! May they repent, turn to you, be healed, and follow you all of the days of their lives. Lord of the harvest, send laborers and unite your people to more productive service! Desirous for the accomplishment of your will, we ask all these things here in your precious Presence, that our Joy be complete.*

****************

I hope that you will consider periodically using the following chapters, for the greater work of deep reflection with the one true Loving God - that he would transform you by the renewing of your mind while he also conforms your heart, soul and mind to his. In it, he will cleanse you of the rubbish of your failures, show you how they were just preparation & sanctification in process and encourage you to keep on going, good and faithful servant.

Written as a devotional, these chapters systematically follow the structure of the prayer Jesus taught us. Please go slowly and be open to the insights and promptings that God will provide you personally today. Please do not "read" these but *ponder* them, asking for wisdom and inquiring of God line-by-line. Worship him as you go, remembering that the Hebrew word for prayer includes a component of simultaneous worship.

This cannot occur if you simply repeat the prayer to him, *thinking* your way through. The Lord looks on the "heart" (1 Samuel 16:7), this is "heart" work. This is also worship.

The insights and promptings that come when we slowly immerse ourselves in God's truth will pertain to the wonder of his Love for us, the experiences and memories of our past, and will give us pause to reflect on what he is bringing to mind for our *becoming* today. It will cause new understandings and sometimes great revelation that (hopefully) will lead to an all-day conversation *with him and in him* that will bring better words and deeds to our interactions today - and Joy and Peace that surpasses understanding.

As we saw in John 17, Jesus asked the Father to root and establish the Father's character and attributes in us as he did then with his *talmidim*. His desire is to lead us through each day in one-ness with him and to grow us to reflect his character and attributes more and more (2 Corinthians 3:18, Romans 8:29). As you recognize character and attributes that are not yet fully manifest in you, ask him to refine you. If you will agree to allow him, he will be faithful to Gently do so – that your Joy may be complete.

As you notice that certain requests are repeated frequently, remember the parable of the Persistent Widow (Luke 18:1-8), Jesus' encouragement to persevere in asking and that we are to come before his throne of grace with confidence. You will find threads of scripture throughout, though not always the specific chapter and verse. If you pull on these threads and look up the related scriptures, Adonai will make them come alive for you. Please be sure to add, revise, customize and personalize this as you go - this is between you and him!

As we agree with him for our sanctification, we will ask him to *be* in our thoughts, that our words and actions accomplish *his* will for us more and more;

in a life well lived, in Peace that surpasses all understanding, with Joy among the sorrows of the living in it and for eternity with him in celebration afterwards.

****************

I am now better able to start each morning from my bed thanking him for the work he did in me in my yesterday, and for the good works he accomplished as he flowed through us. As I continue with the prayer he taught us to pray, each section is a reminding reference of his Love and desire for all of the people in the world. As I once again agree with him for all of us, I continue in thanking him and praising him that today he will again move in every heart, soul and mind for the accomplishment of his will. Acknowledging his continued drawing of all of us closer to himself, I ask for *our participation* in his leading, acceptance of his Love and therefore our living of the Joy-filled life.

I hope you will join me in this and ask for his continued provision for all of us: through his forgiveness and help with our forgiving; through his leading and our overcoming of temptation by the power of his Holy Spirit; and his available deliverance of us from Evil. That his kingdom would come and will would be done fully in your life, the lives of every man, woman and child and that each would come to know and share the great divine agape Love that he has for us. That none should perish (2 Peter 3:9).

As was stated in the introduction:

*By the time he gave them this prayer, he had already taught them the associated lessons multiple times and in multiple ways, each section of the prayer serving as a reminding reference for the great depth of the lessons previously learned. Armed with this brief prayer on their hearts, they would be able to quickly remember and agree with the Father in any moment and be able to humbly respond by the power of the Holy Spirit, in the attitudes of the Beatitudes, with fruit of the Spirit language and actions, always and everywhere. That the <u>Father's</u> will be done on earth as it is in heaven.*

This now becomes our task. If we will walk with him, balanced in our hearts, souls and minds, one with him, him in us and us in him, the prayer he taught us to pray a reminding reference, we will be able to humbly respond with fruit of the Spirit, by the power and presence *of* the Holy Spirit, in the character and attributes of God, loving wholly and loving only, providing the information they need to make their choices without Judgement, Condemnation, Coercion or *Man*ipulation - always and everywhere.

This is a lifetime pursuit, *becoming* more successful each day. As he models these for us, we learn more and more how to model them for others as we communicate with them. *Becoming* more and more like him, we will be more and more Patient with others as he helps us to point out the better way, always offering forgiveness and continually communicating in fruit of the Spirit as he himself does with us. There is great Peace and tremendous Joy *in participating in the bringing of his kingdom on earth as it is in heaven*, him living in us, one with him, in the power of his Presence and in his character and attributes.

*We are collaborators co-operating, him in us spiritually and us in him spiritually, with us in the physical creatively participating with him to bring the spiritual into earthly manifestation. Establishing his kingdom on earth as it is in heaven - in people - his will being done: that all might come to know him, love him and join him, and thereby enter into the Family of God.*
*That none should perish.*

He has prepared everything for you. Come! Be like him!

# *Chapter Eleven*

## Our Father In Heaven,
## Hallowed Be Thy Name

*John 17*

*When Jesus had spoken these words, he lifted up his eyes to heaven, and said,*
*"Father, the hour has come; glorify your Son that the Son may glorify you,*
*2 since you have given him authority over all flesh, to give eternal life to all*
*whom you have given him. 3 And this is eternal life, that they know you, the*
*only true God, and Jesus Christ whom you have sent. 4 I glorified you on earth,*
*having accomplished the work that you gave me to do. 5 And now, Father,*
*glorify me in your own presence with the glory that I had with you before the*
*world existed. 6 "I have manifested (rooted and established) your name*
*(character & attributes) to (in) the people whom you gave me out of the world.*
*Yours they were, and you gave them to me, and they have kept your word.*
*7 Now they know that everything that you have given me is from you. 8 For I*
*have given them the words that you gave me, and they have received them and*
*have come to know in truth that I came from you; and they have believed that*
*you sent me. 9 I am praying for them. I am not praying for the world but for*
*those whom you have given me, for they are yours. 10 All mine are yours, and*
*yours are mine, and I am glorified in them. 11 And I am no longer in the world,*
*but they are in the world, and I am coming to you. Holy Father, keep them in*
*your name (the power of our presence and in our character & attributes),*
*which you have given me, that they may be one, even as we are one. 12 While I*
*was with them, I kept them in your name (character & attributes), which you*
*have given me. I have guarded them, and not one of them has been lost except*
*the son of destruction, that the Scripture might be fulfilled. 13 But now I am*
*coming to you, and these things I speak in the world, that they may have my joy*
*fulfilled in themselves. 14 I have given them your word, and the world has*
*hated them because they are not of the world, just as I am not of the world. 15 I*
*do not ask that you take them out of the world, but that you keep them from the*
*evil one. 16 They are not of the world, just as I am not of the world. 17 Sanctify*
*them in the truth; your word is truth. 18 As you sent me into the world, so I*
*have sent them into the world. 19 And for their sake I consecrate myself, that*
*they also may be sanctified in truth. 20 "I do not ask for these only, but also for*

*those who will believe in me through their word, 21 that they may all be one, just as you, Father, are in me, and I in you, that they also may be in us, so that the world may believe that you have sent me. 22 The glory that you have given me I have given to them, that they may be one even as we are one, 23 I in them and you in me, that they may become perfectly one, so that the world may know that you sent me and loved them even as you loved me. 24 Father, I desire that they also, whom you have given me, may be with me where I am, to see my glory that you have given me because you loved me before the foundation of the world. 25 O righteous Father, even though the world does not know you, I know you, and these know that you have sent me. 26 I made known to them your name (the power of your presence, character & attributes), and I will continue to make it known, that the love with which you have loved me may be in them, and I in them."*

*Praise to you, O God* ***our Father in heaven, hallowed be your name*** *(your Presence, character and attributes)! You are like no other – perfect is your character, your attributes are flawless! You are growing us, to produce in and through us, fruit of the Spirit. You have always been, and will always be, for us! Precious are you; life giver, peace giver, purpose giver, our deliverer!*

*In your goodness you inspire your people to serve others to reflect your love for them, that they might come to know you and love you and trust in your abiding love and care. How precious it is to be loved by you! Give us hearts, souls and minds of abiding love and care like yours!*

*Thank you for the opportunities to learn the differences between our ways and your ways. Thank you for what you did in our lives yesterday. Thank you for what we were able to do with you, together, one with you, being transformed by you. Clarify our thoughts today that our words and actions accomplish your will for us. Made as your imagers, grow us more and more in your perfect loving character and attributes, evident by the fruit of your Spirit flowing through us!*

*Teach us, O Jesus, how to live like you lived and love like you love!*

But how might we *define* love? You may already know that *several* different Greek words are all translated as the *one* English word "*love*". They vary in meaning from human lust, to a heart-felt affection, to God's "agape" or "divine" love.

It is important to note that "agape" is the word that Jesus uses when he gives us the two great "love" commandments. That we love wholly and love only. I have adapted the meaning of agape from BibleTruths.org and HELPS Word-studies:

> Agape is constructive, consistent, active, involved, permanent, given without condition and is willing to sacrifice self for the benefit of another or others. That's a tall order! Agape love is the kind of love that "God is" and that "God prefers" since it is the only kind of love he has for us. For us to love with agape love:
>
> - We *actively* desire to *do* what God "prefers", *with* him, by the power of his Presence and consistent with his character and attributes.
> - As we "prefer" to live and love like Jesus, we will trust his Spirit to lead and guide us, *live through us* and grow us more and more into a reflection of him.
> - Our love will be discriminating and require of us "choice" and "selection" that agrees with his guidance. It will often require *personal sacrifice* that little by little, more and more and glory by glory will conform us to his image (2 Corinthians 3:18, Romans 8:29).
> - As we are transformed by the renewing of our minds (Romans 12:2), these will bring us to "prefer" to love wholly and love only. That what we will say and do will be *acts* of agape in his will.

In the Love Commandments, *love* is the self-sacrificing version. Agape is more than a feeling, *agape takes action*! As was stated previously, Jesus spent three years giving us a *living testimony* of his agape *Love in action*, clarifying for us *how* to do what he *wants us* to do.

We would do well to consider what *we* mean when *we* say "love". Are we describing a lust or desire? A deep heart-felt affection? A love that is so deep that it is willing to sacrifice tremendously for another?

Some confuse love with actions that actually enable bad behaviors to continue. That is not agape! There is a difference between unconditional agape love and *enablement*. Like God, we are to provide the information. Like God, we are to allow others to make their own choices, no matter how Foolish – and continue to love them unconditionally.

The Foolish have a habit of looking for the easy way out, of not truly changing the way they live, and to look for a bailout from those certain people who are confused about the difference between agape love and enablement. Agape love will *strengthen*. Agape love will support the *maturation* of others, and *allow them* to reap the *reward or consequences* of their actions. Agape love does not *save them quickly* and therefore enable the continuation of *Foolish* behavior.

God's Presence in our lives leads us to maturity through the teachings of Jesus, the leading of the Holy Spirit and the works of the Father within us. Our presence in the lives of others should do the same. Help us know the difference, O God, and give us the courage to act accordingly!

***Hallowed be your name!*** *Thank you for your Presence! Thank you that you are active in our hearts and souls and minds that we learn your ways, that we treat those around us in the various expressions of agape love like you, and that you are constantly providing opportunities for us to live out that agape love with you - in Unity together!*

*Thank you that as we are conformed more and more into your image with hearts, souls and minds in balance with you, that you will also strengthen and mature us by your Spirit - that we overcome and "prefer" to love like you. We agree with you and ask that you send more and more laborers.*
*Unite Your people to more productive service!*
***Your kingdom come, your will be done!!!***

# *Chapter Twelve*

## Your Kingdom Come! Your Will Be Done!

On earth as it is in heaven. The whole earth. There is no part of the earth that is excluded. Scripture teaches that the Father sends his rain on the just and the unjust alike. His will is that none should perish. The prayer he taught us to pray is to be for every one of us on the whole earth.

Scripture also teaches that he is active each day in the hearts, souls and minds of every person on earth, drawing all of us to himself that we might know him, love him and find Joy in the abundant life he offers. We will find that Joy when we respond to him, *becoming* one with him, hearing his still small voice in our hearts, souls and minds, doing the will of the Father. That his kingdom would come into the hearts, souls and minds of all – and fill our lives with Joy. Listen for him, he still speaks. He is asking us to *participate* with him, to say and do as he leads – moment by moment. That none should perish.

*John 10:27-29*

*27 <u>My sheep hear my voice, and I know them, and they follow me</u>. 28 I give them eternal life, and they will never perish, and no one will snatch them out of my hand. 29 My Father, who has given them to me, is greater than all, and no one is able to snatch them out of the Father's hand.*

*Jeremiah 29:11-12*

*11 For I know the plans I have for you, declares the Lord, plans for welfare (peace) and not for evil, to give you a future and a hope. 12 <u>Then you will call upon me and come and pray to me, and I will hear you.</u>*

*1 Thessalonians 5:17-18*

*17 pray (inquire, ask, petition, request) <u>without ceasing</u>, 18 give thanks in all circumstances; for this is the will of God in Christ Jesus for you.*

*Isaiah 56:7*

*these I will bring to my holy mountain, <u>and make them joyful in my house of prayer</u>; their burnt offerings and their sacrifices will be accepted on my altar; for my house shall be called <u>a house of prayer for all peoples</u>."*

*Matthew 16:15-17*

*15 He said to them, "But who do you say that I am?" 16 Simon Peter replied, "You are the Christ, the Son of the living God." 17 And Jesus answered him, "Blessed are you, Simon Bar-Jonah! For flesh and blood has not revealed this to you, but my Father who is in heaven.*

*1 Corinthians 6:19*

*Or do you not know that your body is a temple of the Holy Spirit within you, whom you have from God?*

*John 14:10*

*Do you not believe that I am in the Father and the Father is in me? The words that I say to you I do not speak on my own authority, but the Father who dwells in me does his works.*

*Thank you, O Father, that you are within us, whispering to us for our benefit and the benefit of others. Clarify our thoughts, that our words and actions be in accordance with your will for us. Make of us houses of prayer in constant communication with you, in intimate relationship with you, one with you.*

*Psalm 46:10*

*"Be still, and know that I am God. I will be exalted among the nations, I will be exalted in the earth!"*

*John 15:1-5*

*"I am the true vine, and my Father is the vinedresser. 2 Every branch in me that does not bear fruit he takes away, and every branch that does bear fruit he prunes, that it may bear more fruit. 3 Already you are clean because of the word (of the forgiveness) that I have spoken to you. 4 Abide in me, and I in you. As the branch cannot bear fruit by itself, unless it abides in the vine, neither can you, unless you abide in me. 5 I am the vine; you are the branches. Whoever abides in me and I in him, he it is that bears much fruit, for apart from me you can do nothing.*

*Jeremiah 29:13-14*

*13 You will seek me and find me, when you seek me with all your heart. 14 I will be found by you, declares the Lord, and I will restore your fortunes and gather you from all the nations and all the places where I have driven you, declares the Lord, and I will bring you back to the place from which I sent you into exile.*

*Psalm 51:10*
*Create in me a clean heart, O God, and renew a right spirit within me.*

*Psalm 37:4*
*Delight yourself in the Lord, and he will give you the desires of your heart.*

*Matthew 6:33*
*33 But seek first the kingdom of God and his righteousness,*
*and all these things will be added to you.*

*Acts 13:22*
*And when he had removed him (Saul), he raised up David to be their king, of whom he testified and said, 'I have found in David the son of Jesse a man after my heart, who will do all my will.'*

*Ephesians 2:10*
*For we are his workmanship, created in Christ Jesus for good works, which God prepared beforehand, that we should walk in them.*

He has prepared everything for you. Come, talmid, *become* like him! Agree with him that his will be done in your life! He is uniting his people to more productive service, will you join him in this?

*Jehovah (YHWH, I Am Who Am, the Lord Eternal and self existent), Abba (Daddy), El Elohim (the Lord our God and Creator):* ***Your kingdom come, your will be done, on earth as it is in heaven.*** *Adonai (triune God: Father, Son, Holy Spirit), fill us with your Spirit and train us up in your ways. Thank you for replacing our selfish hearts of stone. May our new regenerated hearts be fully after yours, that the desires of our hearts be the desires you have for us. That our will would fully spring from your will for us. Therefore, may whatever we ask here in the power of your Presence and in your character and attributes from our new hearts be what you desire for us to ask. Adonai, make us one as you are one, you in us and us in you, dwell in us and accomplish your works. Keep us always intimate with you, that you grow us to abound in grace, faith, love, mercy, forgiveness, hope and truth. May we abide in you as you abide in us and, like Jesus, only do and say what the Father wills.*

*John 12:49-50*

*49 For I have not spoken on my own authority, but the Father who sent me <u>has himself given me a commandment - what to say and what to speak</u>. 50 And I know that his commandment is eternal life. <u>What I say, therefore, I say as the Father has told me</u>."*

*John 5:19*

*So Jesus said to them, "<u>Truly, truly</u>, I say to you, <u>the Son can do nothing of his own accord</u>, but only what he sees the Father doing. For whatever the Father does, that the Son does likewise.*

*Proverbs 3:3-8*

*3 My son, do not forget my teaching, but <u>let your heart</u> keep my commandments, 2 for length of days and years of life and peace they will add to you. 3 Let not steadfast love and faithfulness forsake you; bind them around your neck; <u>write them on the tablet of your heart</u>. 4 So you will find favor and good success in the sight of God and man. 5 Trust in the Lord <u>with all your heart</u>, and do not lean on your own understanding (mind). 6 In all your ways acknowledge him, and he will make straight your paths. 7 Be not wise in your own eyes (mind); fear the Lord, and turn away from evil. 8 It will be healing to your flesh and refreshment to your bones.*

*John 14:10*

*Do you not believe that I am in the Father and the Father is in me? The words that I say to you <u>I do not speak on my own authority, but the Father who dwells in me does his works</u>.*

*Father, I thank you that you are moving in the hearts, souls and minds of every man, woman and child on the whole earth; that we each have every opportunity to come to know you, love you and trust you – as it is in heaven. Draw us closer and closer to you, strengthening us in love and understanding, that we become more and more like you and one with you. Help us to know your voice, and therefore know what to say and do.*

*Help us know what is ours to do and what is not ours to do. May we not interfere with your will as we see what <u>could</u> be done and assume we must do it! Thank you for the power of your Presence in prayer as <u>you</u> are active in the lives of those to whom we are <u>not</u> to speak or act. Thank you that it is* *sufficient in those times that we simply thank you and praise you for what you are doing and are continuing to do. Thank you for the others whom you are leading to them and leading them to. We ask that you send more laborers and that you Unite us all to more productive service!*

*Thank you for your Peace as we remember that we are not alone.*

*John 15:6-11*

*6 If anyone does not abide in me he is thrown away like a branch and withers; and the branches are gathered, thrown into the fire, and burned. 7 If you abide in me, and my words abide in you, ask whatever you wish, and it will be done for you. 8 By this my Father is glorified, that you bear much fruit and so prove to be my disciples (talmidim). 9 As the Father has loved me, so have I loved you. Abide in my love. 10 If you keep my commandments, you will abide in my love, just as I have kept my Father's commandments and abide in his love. 11 These things I have spoken to you, that my joy may be in you, and that your joy may be full.*

*Colossians 3:5-16a, 17*

*5 Put to death therefore what is earthly in you: sexual immorality, impurity, passion, evil desire, and covetousness, which is idolatry. 6 On account of these the wrath of God is coming. 7 In these you too once walked, when you were living in them. 8 But now you must put them all away: anger, wrath, malice, slander, and obscene talk from your mouth. 9 Do not lie to one another, seeing that you have put off the old self with its practices 10 and have put on the new self, which is being renewed in knowledge after the image of its creator. 11 Here there is not Greek and Jew, circumcised and uncircumcised, barbarian, Scythian, slave, free; but Christ is all, and in all. 12 Put on then, as God's chosen ones, holy and beloved, compassionate hearts, kindness, humility, meekness, and patience, 13 bearing with one another and, if one has a complaint against another, forgiving each other; as the Lord has forgiven you, so you also must forgive. 14 And above all these put on love, which binds everything together in perfect harmony. 15 And let the peace of Christ rule in your hearts, to which indeed you were called in one body. And be thankful. 16 Let the word of Christ dwell in you richly, teaching and admonishing one another in all wisdom, singing psalms and hymns and spiritual songs, with thankfulness in your hearts to God. ...17 And* whatever you do, in word or deed, do everything in the name (in the power of his presence and in the character and attributes) of the Lord Jesus, giving thanks to God the Father through him.

Galatians 5:16-24

16 But I say, walk by the Spirit, and you will not gratify the desires of the
flesh. 17 For the desires of the flesh are against the Spirit, and the desires of
the Spirit are against the flesh, for these are opposed to each other, to keep
you from doing the things you want to do. 18 But if you are led by the Spirit,
you are not under the law. 19 Now the works of the flesh are evident: sexual
immorality, impurity, sensuality, 20 idolatry, sorcery, enmity, strife, jealousy,
fits of anger, rivalries, dissensions, divisions, 21 envy, drunkenness, orgies,
and things like these. I warn you, as I warned you before, that those who
(continue to) do such things will not inherit the kingdom of God. 22 But the
fruit of the Spirit is love, joy, peace, patience, kindness, goodness,
faithfulness, 23 gentleness, self-control; against such things there is no law.
24 And those who belong to Christ Jesus have crucified the flesh
with its passions and desires.

---

We agree with you, Adonai (triune God: Father, Son, Holy Spirit); that we be one as you are one - you in us and us in you - that **your kingdom come and your will be done on earth as it is in heaven**. Therefore, O God, convert our hearts and place your desires for us within them. Therefore, transform us by the renewing of our minds. Therefore, clarify our thoughts, that our words and actions be in accordance with your will for us. Therefore, bind and loose on earth as in heaven, according to your will. Therefore, teach us, train us, guide us, Unite us to more productive service in your ways and in your will, one with you. Therefore, give us Wisdom, Self-Control, Perseverance and Patience that we be reliable witnesses reflecting your glory in the various expressions of agape Love. Thank you for your Peace as we remember that it is you who is bringing your kingdom and that we are given the privilege of participating in it with you. Thank you for the Joy of seeing you in action. With us, in us and through us!

Ephesians 6:10-18

10 Finally, be strong in the Lord and in the strength of his might. 11 Put on
the whole armor of God, that you may be able to stand against the schemes

*of the devil. 12 For we do not wrestle against flesh and blood, but against the rulers, against the authorities, against the cosmic powers over this present darkness, against the spiritual forces of evil in the heavenly places.*
*13 Therefore take up the whole armor of God, that you may be able to withstand in the evil day, and having done all, to stand firm. 14 Stand therefore, having fastened on the belt of truth, and having put on the breastplate of righteousness, 15 and, as shoes for your feet, having put on the readiness given by the gospel of peace. 16 In all circumstances take up the shield of faith, with which you can extinguish all the flaming darts of the evil one; 17 and take the helmet of salvation, and the sword of the Spirit, which is the word of God, 18 praying at all times in the Spirit, with all prayer and supplication. To that end, keep alert with all perseverance, making supplication for all the saints.*

*Give us insight into the ways in which we fail you. Help us to realize the impact our ways are having on the lives of others today, and how our ways are affecting future lives in big picture ways. Teach us that we perceive how our ways are blocking the coming of your kingdom today and are rebellion against your will for us. Train us up in your ways, O God!*

*El Shaddai (the All Sufficient One): You are our greatest need. All we need may be found in you. All we need to accomplish your will for us today is being provided by you; Jehovah Shalom (the Lord is our Peace - even under great pressure), thank you for your Peace as we remember that.*

# *Chapter Thirteen*

## Give Us This Day Our Daily Bread

How big is your "us"? My tendency is that it includes my family and friends, but Jesus tells us to pray for all of the people on the earth. That all of us will receive our daily bread.

*Thank you, Father, for big prayers. Praying big helps keep me from thinking small, with a focus upon self, when millions are without food and clean water.*

*We ask you for the whole world, and the leaders of every nation. We understand that there is a battle going on between you and your Enemies for all the nations. Between your nations and the Enemy's nations.*
*Give us Wisdom in our actions, O God!*

*Nevertheless, we are <u>all</u> your people, Adonai, in the process of Accepting you or Rejecting you – person by person and nation by nation. Thank you for helping us to keep our eyes on you and the big picture, rather than on me and my small world.*

*Matthew 6:25-26*
*25 "Therefore I tell you, <u>do not be anxious</u> about your life, what you will eat or*
*what you will drink, nor about your body, what you will put on. Is not life more*
*than food, and the body more than clothing? 26 Look at the birds of the air:*
*they neither sow nor reap nor gather into barns, and yet your heavenly Father*
*feeds them. Are you not of more value than they?*

*Matthew 6:28-30*
*28 And <u>why are you anxious</u> about clothing? Consider the lilies of the field,*
*how they grow: they neither toil nor spin, 29 yet I tell you, even Solomon in all*
*his glory was not arrayed like one of these. 30 But if God so clothes the grass*
*of the field, which today is alive and tomorrow is thrown into the oven, will he*
*not much more clothe you, O you of little faith?*

*Matthew 6:31-33*
*31 Therefore <u>do not be anxious</u>, saying, 'What shall we eat?' or 'What shall we*
*drink?' or 'What shall we wear?' 32 For the Gentiles seek after all these*

*things, and your heavenly Father knows that you need them all. 33 <u>But seek first the kingdom of God and his righteousness, and all these things will be added to you</u>.*

---

*Jehovah Jireh (the Lord will provide):* ***Give*** *all of* ***us this day our daily bread****, in communion with you. Thank you for your care and provision of both physical and spiritual food. May this be an entire day of communion with you, receiving from you and pouring out what you have given to us for the support of others and in support of your purpose in this world, according to your will. Not according to a sense of guilt, or desire to control for you, but according to your clear promptings - with you. You have made your provision for all available through us. May we release your provision, O God!*

*Matthew 25:35*
*For I was hungry and you gave me food, I was thirsty and you gave me drink, I was a stranger and you welcomed me,*

*Proverbs 19:17*
*Whoever is generous to the poor lends to the Lord,*
*and he will repay him for his deed.*

*Proverbs 21:13*
*Whoever closes his ear to the cry of the poor will himself call out*
*and not be answered.*

*Proverbs 14:31*
*Whoever oppresses a poor man insults his Maker,*
*but he who is generous to the needy honors him.*

*James 1:27*
*Religion that is pure and undefiled before God the Father is this: to visit orphans and widows in their affliction, and to keep oneself unstained from the world.*

*Job 29:12*
*because I delivered the poor who cried for help,*
*and the fatherless who had none to help him.*

---

*Deuteronomy 15:11*

*For there will never cease to be poor in the land. Therefore I command you, 'You shall open wide your hand to your brother, to the needy and to the poor, in your land.'*

*1 John 3:17-18*

*17 But if anyone has the world's goods and sees his brother in need, yet closes his heart against him, how does God's love abide in him? 18 Little children, let us not love in word or talk but in deed and in truth.*

*Acts 10:4b*

*"What is it, Lord?" And he said to him, "Your prayers and your alms have ascended as a memorial before God.*

*Matthew 25:31-46 The Final Judgment*

*31 "When the Son of Man comes in his glory, and all the angels with him, then he will sit on his glorious throne. 32 Before him will be gathered all the nations, and he will separate people one from another as a shepherd separates the sheep from the goats. 33 And he will place the sheep on his right, but the goats on the left. 34 Then the King will say to those on his right, 'Come, you who are blessed by my Father, inherit the kingdom prepared for you from the foundation of the world. 35 For I was hungry and you gave me food, I was thirsty and you gave me drink, I was a stranger and you welcomed me, 36 I was naked and you clothed me, I was sick and you visited me, I was in prison and you came to me.' 37 Then the righteous will answer him, saying, 'Lord, when did we see you hungry and feed you, or thirsty and give you drink? 38 And when did we see you a stranger and welcome you, or naked and clothe you? 39 And when did we see you sick or in prison and visit you?' 40 And the King will answer them, 'Truly, I say to you, as you did it to one of the least of these my brothers, you did it to me.' 41 "Then he will say to those on his left, 'Depart from me, you cursed, into the eternal fire prepared for the devil and his angels. 42 For I was hungry and you gave me no food, I was thirsty and you gave me no drink, 43 I was a stranger and you did not welcome me, naked and you did not clothe me, sick and in prison and you did not visit me.' 44 Then they also will answer, saying, 'Lord, when did we see you hungry or thirsty or a stranger or naked or sick or in prison, and did not minister to you?' 45 Then he will answer them, saying, 'Truly, I say to you, as you did not*

*do it to one of the least of these, you did not do it to me.' 46 And these will go away into eternal punishment,*
*but the righteous into eternal life."*

*May the whole world be fed today, O God. Show us the way to your provision that we all have enough every day! You have heard the cries of your people. Unite us to more productive service, give us relief from our Adversaries and send more laborers for the accomplishment of your will!*

*As others receive their daily bread from you through us may we reflect your glory and give you all praise. Give us wisdom in the use of what you have given us, for we have given it all back to you for your use! All we are and all we have are yours, O God! May we not fail you and overspend your riches on ourselves when your intention is that we would bless others and advance your purpose in this world. May we share what you have given us with others according to your will and in tune with your timing, pointing them to you and for your glory. Unite your people in more productive service! Desirous for the accomplishment of your will, we ask all these things here in your precious Presence, that our Joy be complete.*

*Luke 11:11-13*

*11 What father among you, if his son asks for a fish, will instead of a fish give him a serpent; 12 or if he asks for an egg, will give him a scorpion? 13 If you then, who are evil, know how to give good gifts to your children, <u>how much more will the heavenly Father give the Holy Spirit to those who ask him</u>!"*

*Isaiah 60:17*

*Instead of bronze I will bring gold, and instead of iron I will bring silver; instead of wood, bronze, instead of stones, iron. <u>I will make your overseers peace and your taskmasters righteousness</u>.*

*Wonderful Counselor, gracious God: Refresh us again today, filling us with the Bread of Heaven. May we share your Bread of Life and Living Water with others according to your will for us. Thank you that you will move in all our hearts and souls and minds again today, drawing us to you and strengthening us. Dwell in us and accomplish your works. May we be fully aware and attentive to your Presence that you produce your fruit through us.*

*You are the Vine, providing Love, Joy, Peace, Patience (a willingness for long-suffering for your purpose), Kindness, Goodness, Perseverance (faithfulness, steadfastness), Gentleness and Self-Control to and through us, the branches. May we no longer Judge, Condemn, Coerce, Demand, Deceive or Shame in an attempt to Control others. To make happen what we want to have happen, for our purposes. Rather, lead us to encourage, share, explain, train, inform, coach and describe in your Kindness and with your Gentleness, in your ways, in Unity with your purpose - and give us ears to hear as well! Unite your people in more productive service, O God!*

*Proverbs 6:16-19*

*16 There are six things that the Lord hates, seven that are an abomination to him: 17 haughty eyes, a lying tongue, and hands that shed innocent blood, 18 a heart that devises wicked plans, feet that make haste to run to evil, 19 a false witness who breathes out lies, and one who sows discord among brothers.*

*Matthew 5:2-12 The fruit of humility*

*2 And he opened his mouth and taught them, saying: 3 "Blessed are the poor in spirit, for theirs is the kingdom of heaven. 4 "Blessed are those who mourn, for they shall be comforted. 5 "Blessed are the meek, for they shall inherit the earth. 6 "Blessed are those who hunger and thirst for righteousness, for they shall be satisfied. 7 "Blessed are the merciful, for they shall receive mercy. 8 "Blessed are the pure in heart, for they shall see God. 9 "Blessed are the peacemakers, for they shall be called sons of God. 10 "Blessed are those who are persecuted for righteousness' sake, for theirs is the kingdom of heaven. 11 "Blessed are you when others revile you and persecute you and utter all kinds of evil against you falsely on my account. 12 Rejoice and be glad, for your reward is great in heaven, for so they persecuted the prophets who were before you.*

*Matthew 5:43-48*

*Even the evil: Persevering Love and Humility are Foundational*

*43 "You have heard that it was said, 'You shall love your neighbor and hate your enemy.' 44 But I say to you, <u>Love your enemies and pray for those who persecute you,</u> 45 so that you may be sons of your Father who is in heaven. For he makes his sun rise on the evil and on the good, and sends rain on the just* *and on the unjust. 46 For if you love those who love you, what reward do you have? Do not even the tax collectors do the same? 47 And if you greet only your brothers, what more are you doing than others? Do not even the Gentiles do the same? 48 You therefore must be perfect, as your heavenly Father is perfect.*

---

*Thank you, Father, for doing your works in us. Thank you that you are perfecting us little by little, glory by glory (2 Corinthians 3:18). Thank you, Jesus, that the Father sees us as perfected in you. Thank you, Spirit, for your voice leading and guiding us in the will of the Father. May we always remember the allure of the Enemy towards Selfishness and Depravity and not enter into temptation. Lead us and guide us in your ways that we accomplish your will for us in the lives of those who are so clueless about you! Strengthen us, O God, as we participate with you in drawing them home!*

*Isaiah 1:2-5, 15-21a, 23*

*2 Hear, O heavens, and give ear, O earth; for the Lord has spoken: "Children have I reared and brought up, but they have rebelled against me. 3 The ox knows its owner, and the donkey its master's crib, but Israel does not know, my people do not understand." 4 Ah, sinful nation, a people laden with iniquity, offspring of evildoers, children who deal corruptly! They have forsaken the Lord, they have despised the Holy One of Israel, they are utterly estranged. 5 Why will you still be struck down? Why will you continue to rebel? The whole head is sick, and the whole heart faint. ...15 When you spread out your hands, I will hide my eyes from you; even though you make many prayers, I will not listen; your hands are full of blood. 16 Wash yourselves; make yourselves clean; remove the evil of your deeds from before my eyes; cease to do evil, 17 learn to do good; seek justice, correct oppression; bring justice to the fatherless, plead the widow's cause. 18 "Come now, let us reason together, says the Lord: though your sins are like scarlet, they shall be as white as snow; though they are red like crimson, they shall become like wool. 19 If you are willing and obedient, you shall eat the good of the land; 20 but if you refuse and rebel, you shall be eaten by the sword; for the mouth of the Lord has spoken." 21a How the faithful city has become a whore, (become unchaste) she who was full of justice!... 23 Your princes are rebels and companions of thieves. Everyone loves a bribe and runs after gifts. They do not bring justice to the fatherless, and the widow's cause does not come to them.*

---

*Thank you that, whatever is before us, we know that our clear responsibility is to respond humbly with fruit of the Spirit in the attitudes of Jesus. You are the Vine, providing Love, Joy, Peace, Patience (a willingness for long-suffering for your purpose), Kindness, Goodness, Perseverance (faithfulness, steadfastness), Gentleness and Self-Control to and through us, the branches.*

*Give us Wisdom, that we avoid Judgement and Condemnation, or choose to Manipulate or Coerce to try to gain or regain Control. Though we have all learned these behaviors from the world around us, by the power of your Presence and in your character and attributes, may we always respond as you do with us – with information in the fruit of the Spirit – and freely allow others to make their choice. As you do with us.*

*1 Thessalonians 5:19*
*Do not quench the Spirit.*

*Matthew 18:2-6*
*2 And calling to him a child, he put him in the midst of them 3 and said, "Truly, I say to you, unless you turn and become like children, you will never enter the kingdom of heaven. 4 Whoever humbles himself like this child is the greatest in the kingdom of heaven. 5 "Whoever receives one such child in my name (according to my character and attributes) receives me, 6 but whoever causes one of these little ones who believe in me to sin, it would be better for him to have a great millstone fastened around his neck and to be drowned in the depth of the sea.*

*Proverbs 22:6*
*Train up a child in the way he should go; even when he is old he will not depart from it.*

*Ephesians 6:4*
*4 Fathers, do not provoke your children to anger, but bring them up in the discipline and instruction of the Lord.*

*Exodus 20:5-6*
*You shall not worship them or serve them; for I, the Lord your God, am a jealous God, visiting the iniquity of the fathers on the children, on the third and the fourth generations of those who hate Me, but showing loving kindness to thousands, to those who love Me and keep My commandments.*

*Numbers 14:18*

*'The Lord is slow to anger and abundant in loving kindness, forgiving iniquity and transgression; but He will by no means clear the guilty, visiting the iniquity of the fathers on the children to the third and the fourth generations.'*

*Jeremiah 32:17-19*

*17 'Ah, Lord God! It is you who have made the heavens and the earth by your
great power and by your outstretched arm! Nothing is too hard for you. 18 You
show steadfast love to thousands, but you repay the guilt of fathers to their
children after them, O great and mighty God, whose name is the Lord of hosts,
19 great in counsel and mighty in deed, whose eyes are open to all the ways of
the children of man, rewarding each one according to his ways and according
to the fruit of his deeds.*

*Luke 16:10-13*

*10 "One who is faithful in a very little is also faithful in much, and one who is
dishonest in a very little is also dishonest in much. 11 If then you have not been
faithful in the unrighteous wealth, who will entrust to you the true riches?
12 And if you have not been faithful in that which is another's, who will give
you that which is your own? 13 No servant can serve two masters, for either he
will hate the one and love the other, or he will be devoted to the one and
despise the other. You cannot serve God and money."*

*Proverbs 16:25*

*There is a way that seems right to a man, but its end is the way to death.*

*Mark 10:15*

*Truly, I say to you, whoever does not receive the kingdom of God <u>like a child</u> shall not enter it."*

---

*Father, thank you that your Holy Spirit leads us and guides us. The tremendous complexity of the workings of this world are too much for us to figure out with our minds. Thank you that we may come to you like little children, asking for your Wisdom and Direction. Thank you that you are available for that unceasingly, and that you actually desire that we do so continually.*

*Thank you that you are moving in the hearts, souls and minds of every person in every nation. As you awaken us, may we be attentive to you. That our nation, that all nations, not come under condemnation, but instead govern your people as one with you and therefore in your righteousness.*

*Do not turn your hand against us, O God, but rather make of us a people that love as you Love, live as you Live and bring you glory. We see Corruption in the people Directing our governments, lead them that they abandon their pursuit of power, come to know you, love you, trust you and do your will - or replace them with people of your own! Send laborers, O God, that our Adversaries turn, repent and accomplish <u>your</u> will! We are suffering according to the power we have given those in so many forms of governance. There is so much more we have to do to support and protect all people. In your grace and mercy, show us our way to restoration through the discipline you will bring for our benefit.*

*Jehova Repheka (the Lord is our Healer, based on our obedience): When things are not going our way we try to gain Control by making Demands and Judgments that Coerce, by expressing Blame, Anger and Condemnation that Threaten - Manipulating to get what we want - Dividing one against another that sides may be taken in support of our will, for what we think best - but that way leads to death. Develop in us ears that hear your voice and hearts and minds obedient to <u>your</u> Direction - that you heal us!*

***Forgive us our sin**, O God, that so many are impoverished across the world, without healthy food and clean water. Great is your provision for all! Make us one as you are one, you in us and us in you, that together we may generously share the time, resources, care and compassion that you have first given us. That none should perish for lack of food and water. That none should perish for the lack of knowing your Love. Give us justice against our Adversaries, O God! May they repent, turn to you, be healed, and follow you all of the days of their lives. Lord of the harvest, send laborers, unite Your people to more productive service! Desirous for the accomplishment of your will, we ask all these things here in your precious Presence, that our Joy be complete.*

# *Chapter Fourteen*

## Forgive Us Our Sin As We Forgive Others

How big is your "us"? My tendency is that it includes my family and friends, but Jesus tells us to pray for all of the people on the earth. That all of us will forgive and be forgiven. Forgiven, forgiving, for giving, for living.

I need to continually accept God's training with regard to my failings in my "yesterdays," and I had better be open to him and aware of them while they are still fresh in my mind "today". He is Gentle with me in this, and he will be Gentle with you, too. It's one of his character traits and an attribute that we can acquire for the benefit of others.

If you ponder in humility, you will find opportunities to inquire of him regarding every aspect of your life. As you are open to the Holy Spirit, expect him to stop you, his talmid, along the way to expand upon the practical applications for your life today. With your assent, he will increasingly transform you into his likeness and conform you to his character & attributes (Romans 8:29 and 2 Corinthians 3:18) for the people with whom you will interact today - his words and actions through you. Please pray in agreement with him for these things, *that his kingdom will come and his will will be done in your day.*

In John 13:34-35, Jesus gave us one more commandment, *"A new commandment I give to you, that you love one another: just as I have loved you, you also are to love one another. By this all people will know that you are my disciples (talmidim), if you have love for one another."* To love wholly and love only we need to agree with the Holy Spirit to will and to do in our hearts, souls and minds – and therefore in our lives. To conform us, to transform us, to grow us, to change us and to bring to us the abundant life - that our Joy may be full. (John 15:9-11, John 17:13)

*Romans 12:1-2*

*1 I appeal to you therefore, brothers, by the mercies of God, to present your bodies as a living sacrifice, holy and acceptable to God, which is your spiritual worship. 2 Do not be conformed to this world, but be transformed by the renewal of your mind, that by testing you may discern what is the will of God, what is good and acceptable and perfect.*

*Micah 6:8*
*8 He has told you, O man, what is good; and what does the Lord require of you but to do justice, and to love kindness, and to walk humbly with your God?*

*Colossians 3:12-15*
*12 Put on then, as God's chosen ones, holy and beloved, compassionate hearts, kindness, humility, meekness, and patience, 13 bearing with one another and, if one has a complaint against another, forgiving each other; as the Lord has forgiven you, so you also must forgive. 14 And above all these put on love, which binds everything together in perfect harmony. 15 And let the peace of Christ rule in your hearts, to which indeed you were called in one body. And be thankful.*

*Psalm 23:6*
*Surely goodness and mercy shall follow me (characterize me) all the days of my life, and I shall dwell in the house of the Lord forever.*

At the time of the great celebration of the completion of the temple, King Solomon asked God what he would do in the future when they had forgotten this day, their previous faithfulness, and had each gone off in their own way - causing his discipline to come upon them. God continues to be true to the promise he made that day as written in 2 Chronicles 7:12-14:

*12 Then the Lord appeared to Solomon in the night and said to him: "I have heard your prayer and have chosen this place for myself as a house of sacrifice. 13 When I shut up the heavens so that there is no rain, or command the locust to devour the land, or send pestilence among my people, 14 if my people who are called by my name (called to live in the power of my presence and in my character and attributes) humble themselves, and pray and seek my face (inquire of me for my will) and turn from their wicked ways, then I will hear from heaven and will forgive their sin and heal their land.*

*Jehovah Rophe (the Lord heals, who is our Healer): May we humbly pray and seek your face & turn from our wicked ways (Pride, Blame, Judgment, Condemnation, Anger, Resentment, Vengeance, Coercion, subtle Manipulation, Deception, Shaming, efforts to Control, Retribution, Selfishness and Refusals to give, Accusation, Rationalization, Lies, Retaliation, Lust, Trickery, Excess,*

*Covetousness, Abuse of Power). O Spirit Of The Living God, please replace all darkness within us with you, make us one as you are one, you in us and us in you and humbly produce fruit of the Spirit - Love, Joy, Peace, Patience (a willingness for long-suffering for your purpose), Kindness, Goodness, Perseverance (faithfulness, steadfastness), Gentleness and Self-Control. Accomplish your will for us! In the attitudes of the Beatitudes, strengthen our faith, hope, humility, Love. Heal our hearts, our souls, our minds, our bodies, our families, our land, our lives, our country, our world. Unite your people in more productive service, O God!*

*Train us up in your ways, O God. Jehovah Maccadeshem (the Lord who sanctifies and sweetens), sanctify us and sweeten us. Prompt us to encourage, share, explain, train, inform, coach and describe with your Gentleness, in your ways and in Unity with your purpose – without Manipulation! O Potter, reshape us as you would have us, transform us by the renewing of our minds and the conversion of our hearts - evident by the fruit of the Spirit in us, the character and attributes of God in us, producing Love, Joy, Peace, Patience (a willingness for long-suffering for your purpose), Kindness, Goodness, Perseverance (faithfulness, steadfastness), Gentleness and Self-Control - reflecting your glory.*

*Jehovah Sabbaoth (the Lord of Hosts, when his children have failed he will keep all his promises), Abba (Daddy):* ***Thank you for your forgiveness of our failings each day!*** *Train us up in your ways that we follow your forgiveness and keep our promises with those who fail us each day. Let us not be tempted to continue in our ways or return to our former ways. Clarify our thoughts, that our words and actions accomplish your will for us, one with you, you in us and us in you. Dwell in us, Father, and do your works.*
*Not my will, but your will be done.*

***Forgive us our sins as we forgive those who sin against us.*** *If we are unforgiving, or forgive with subtle Coercion to try to Manipulate and Control people, how can we expect your forgiveness? Teach us to forgive like you, graciously and without Manipulation.*

***Forgive us our trespasses as we forgive those who trespass against us.*** *Forgive us for crossing the line and pressuring people to do what we want. May we also forgive others who do the same to us. The difference between*

*Dictatorial regimes and our Manipulative ways is only a matter of scale and degree. Teach us and train us to recognize when we are being tempted to Coerce or Manipulate others that we may instead learn to offer, share, describe and explain our position without Malice, Coercion, Manipulation or Veiled Threat.*

**Forgive us our debts as we forgive our debtors.** *We are indebted to you for our very lives. All that we have has come from you, but you do not call it debt, rather your gift. We have been blessed by you not so much to have, but to be able to also give, and generously!*

*You do not demand our love in return. That would be Manipulative and Coercive. Rather, we are free to choose to love you or to not love you. Forgive us when we make Demands of others for what we think they owe us, for what we think they should do, because of what we want them to do. Train us to give them the freedom to return our love or not, to give back to us or not to give back to us – as you have done with us. In their freedom to choose, may they not choose Selfishly but recognize your Love in us being given to them – and turn to you for strength to do the same. May we each decide to give love as you give Love – unconditionally!*

*Forgive us when we overspend your riches on goods for ourselves and when we enslave ourselves to debts that rob us of our freedom to be generous – both with time and money. Help us to liberate ourselves that we may experience once again the Joy of giving generously to others and in the helping of the less fortunate all around us.*

***Forgive us for what we have left undone.*** *Forgive us for our Selfishness as we withhold what we are able to give. May we give as you give – generously! May we not be so busy with the demands of the day that we fail to share quality time, but instead give the best of ourselves to the ones most dear to us. May we remember that agape Love involves action, is more than just a feeling, and not just something that we "have". May we Love you with all our heart, with all our soul, with all our mind and with all our strength, and Love our neighbor as our self. May we Love one another as you have Loved us. By this, all people will know that we are yours, are becoming more like you and are being drawn to come to know you, too.*

*Teach us how to give Love rather than withhold it so as to subtly Coerce. Train us up in your ways so that we learn how to both give Love and caringly point out the better way. Give us Wisdom, that we be merciful, gracious and giving like you. In your grace and mercy, remember your promises – as well, may we!*

*Move in our hearts, overcome our minds and show us how to forgive those whom we have not forgiven. There is nothing that we have done that you are not willing to forgive. The depth of our darkness is known to you. The depth of our Depravity, Aggression, Violence, and Shame are as scarlet, but you offer to remember them no more. In the same way, there is nothing others have done to us that is unforgiveable.*

*Jehova Repheka (the Lord is our Healer, based on our obedience) forgive us our failures as we forgive those who have failed us. Forgive us the pain we have caused others in the same way that we forgive the pain that others have caused us. Forgive us our rebellion against you just like we forgive those who rebel against us. Forgive us our betrayals of you according to the way we forgive those who betray us.*

*Isaiah 30:15 NIV*
*This is what the Sovereign Lord, the Holy One of Israel, says: "In repentance and rest is your salvation, in quietness and trust is your strength, but you would have none of it.*

*Adonai, thank you that you will show us our way to Peace and forgiveness and intimate relationship with you if we will but turn from trying to Control our lives ourselves, trust in you for our forgiveness and salvation and be led by your Spirit. Thank you that in repentance and rest is our salvation, your salve for our sorrow and your salve for our souls. Thank you for the strength given by you in quietness and in trusting you for it all. Thank you for giving us the strength to forgive others and remember their sin no more. Thank you that you bring healing to relationships and Peace to the soul.*

*Jehovah Rophe (the Lord heals, who is our Healer): May we humbly turn from our wicked ways (Pride, Blame, Judgment, Condemnation, Anger, Resentment, Vengeance, Coercion, subtle Manipulation, Deception, Shaming, efforts to Control, Retribution, Selfishness & Refusals to give, Accusation,*

*Rationalization, Lies, Retaliation, Lust, Trickery, Excess, Covetousness, Abuse of Power) by the power of your Holy Spirit.*

*Isaiah 53:6*
*All we like sheep have gone astray;*
*we have turned - every one - to his own way;*
*and the Lord has laid on him the iniquity of us all.*

---

*Thank you, Jesus, for your great sacrifice on our behalf! O Spirit Of The Living God, please replace all darkness within us with you, make us one as you are one, you in us and us in you, humbly producing fruit of the Spirit - Love, Joy, Peace, Patience (a willingness for long-suffering for your purpose), Kindness, Goodness, Perseverance (faithfulness, steadfastness), Gentleness and Self-Control. Accomplish your will for us! In the attitudes of the Beatitudes, strengthen our faith, hope, humility, ability and capacity to Love.*

***Heal our hearts, our souls, our minds, our bodies, our families, our land, our lives, our country, our world. We ask that you give us relief from our Adversaries and send more laborers for the benefit of all of us, that all come into Joyful relationship with you. Unite us all in more productive service, O God!***

# The Fruit of the Spirit & The Whole Armor of God in Conflict Resolution

*"In this world you will have trouble." (John 16:33)*

What do we do with the trouble before us? How do we present it to those involved?

The fruit of the Spirit are God's reference points for our behavior & the tools with which we are to contend. The whole armor of God is our protection when others attack us, absorbing the blows and taking the arrows *for* us. So love like He does and communicate like He does, knowing full well that they may choose to go their own way - and continue to lean on their own understanding. It may also be that *we* are the ones responding in Fear of losing control, and not with the respectful Wisdom that shares information for our mutual benefit. Often God's help is in the overlap, somewhere between our oppositions, and available for discernment.

There is a difference between unconditional love and enablement. Like God, we are to provide the information. Like God, we are to allow others to make their own choice, no matter how foolish - and continue to love them unconditionally. One of the expressions of that love is to allow them to go out and learn on their own what they have chosen not to learn from the wisdom of others. When we love unconditionally, we bathe them in prayer when they go their own way, asking God to intervene that they may *learn quickly*. Enablement *saves them quickly* such that they *learn little* and so *continue to repeat their folly*.

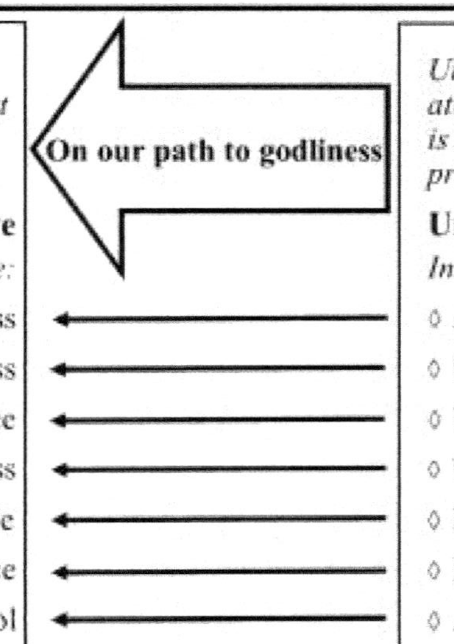


*Unity Builders produce fruit of the Spirit in an attempt to create or maintain unity during conflict resolution. Respectful information sharing, care, and a relational focus are the motivating factors.*

**Unity Builders: In Humility & Love**

*The Spirit of the Lord offers freedom, so we:*

- ◊ Inform with Gentleness
- ◊ Encourage with Kindness
- ◊ Explain with grace in Peace
- ◊ Share with compassion in Goodness
- ◊ Describe with hope the Joyful outcome available
- ◊ Train to produce Patience & Perseverance
- ◊ Coach to develop Self-Control

*Unity Busters accuse, judge, condemn and shame people in an attempt to maintain or retake control over a situation. The focus is Autonomy & Control of others. Over time, this manipulation produces relational loss.*

**Unity Busters: In Fear of Loss**

*In our attempt to Control, we:*

- ◊ Accuse, Judge & Condemn to Justify our Demands
- ◊ Use Blame, Anger and Malice to Threaten and Coerce
- ◊ Use Shame & Silence to subtly Threaten Abandonment
- ◊ Use our Voice to Threaten Vengeance, Retaliation, Retribution
- ◊ Rationalize that our divisive actions were caused by them
- ◊ In Pride & frustration, Lie & Deceive (…for their own good)
- ◊ Abuse whatever Power we may think we have

# Chapter Fifteen

## Lead Us That We Do Not Enter Into Temptation

How big is your "us"? My tendency is that it includes my family and friends, but Jesus tells us to pray for all of the people on the earth. That by the power of the Holy Spirit we all overcome temptation.

*Genesis 4:7*

*7 If you do well, will you not be accepted? And if you do not do well, sin is crouching at the door. Its desire is contrary to you, but you must rule over it."*

*Luke 22:31-32*

*31 "Simon, Simon, behold, Satan demanded to have you, that he might sift you like wheat, 32 but I have prayed (asked the Father) for you that your faith may not fail. And when you have turned again, strengthen your brothers."*

*1 Thessalonians 5:13b-18*

*Be at peace among yourselves. 14 And we urge you, brothers, admonish the idle, encourage the fainthearted, help the weak, be patient with them all. 15 See that no one repays anyone evil for evil, but always seek to do good to one another and to everyone. 16 Rejoice always, 17 pray without ceasing, 18 give thanks in all circumstances; for this is the will of God in Christ Jesus for you.*

*Luke 22:39-40; 45-46*

*39 And he came out and went, as was his custom, to the Mount of Olives, and the disciples (talmidim) followed him. 40 And when he came to the place, he said to them, "Pray that you may not enter into temptation." ... 45 And when he rose from prayer, he came to the disciples (talmidim) and found them sleeping for sorrow, 46 and he said to them, "Why are you sleeping? Rise and pray that you may not enter into temptation."*

*Jehovah Shamah (the Lord is present, everywhere, all the time), El Roi (God, the strong one who sees), Jehovah Rohi/Jehovah Raah (the Lord is my Shephard), Emmanuel (God with us):* ***Lead us*** *that we accomplish your will for*

*us. Lead us that we* ***not*** *enter* ***into temptation*** *to do our own will,* ***but*** *having been prepared and strengthened by you,* ***deliver us from Evil****. By the power of your Holy Spirit, accomplish* <u>*your*</u> *will for us. Jesus told us that he does nothing of his own accord, but only according to the Father's leading.*
*May it be true of us, O God!*

Like Judas, we have been guilty of imagining what we think to be right and then making our attempt to force it to happen. Judas was likely a zealot, from a group called The Zealots, a people passionate for throwing out their Roman occupiers. Like Judas, we are all politicians, *Man*euvering to some degree for what we think would be best. In our zeal, passion and arrogance, we think we know better than others what must be done. Like Judas, we think that if we can initiate the first thing, the thing we want to have happen will then follow. Though Judas believed that the angels would come down from heaven to protect Jesus when they tried to take him away, that the battle for Jerusalem would then be waged against the Romans, that the Romans would then be defeated and Jesus crowned King - it did not happen:

*Matthew 26:47*
*While he was still speaking, Judas came, one of the twelve, and with him a great crowd with swords and clubs, from the chief priests and the elders of the people.*

*Luke 22:47*
*While he was still speaking, there came a crowd, and the man called Judas, one of the twelve, was leading them. He drew near to Jesus to kiss him, but Jesus said to him, "Judas, would you betray the Son of Man with a kiss?"*

*Luke 22:52-53*
*52 Then Jesus said to the chief priests and officers of the temple and elders, who had come out against him, "Have you come out as against a robber, with swords and clubs? 53 When I was with you day after day in the temple, you did not lay hands on me. But this is your hour, and the power of darkness."*

*Matthew 27:1-2*

*1 When morning came, all the chief priests and the elders of the people took counsel against Jesus to put him to death. 2 And they bound him and led him away and delivered him over to Pilate the governor.*

*Matthew 27:3-5*

*3 Then when Judas, his betrayer, saw that Jesus was condemned, he changed his mind and brought back the thirty pieces of silver to the chief priests and the elders, 4 saying, "I have sinned by betraying innocent blood." They said, "What is that to us? See to it yourself." 5 And throwing down the pieces of silver into the temple, he departed, and he went and hanged himself.*

Like Peter, we have seen what we believe should not happen and made our attempt to stop it from occurring. Our will our way, not God's will his way.

*Matthew 16:21-23*

*21 From that time Jesus began to show his disciples that he must go to Jerusalem and suffer many things from the elders and chief priests and scribes, and be killed, and on the third day be raised. 22 And Peter took him aside and began to rebuke him, saying, "<u>Far be it from you, Lord! This shall never happen to you.</u>" 23 But he turned and said to Peter, "Get behind me, Satan! You are a hindrance to me. For you are not setting your mind on the things of God, but on the things of man."*

Then, seeing he had still not learned his lesson, Jesus warned him that he was at risk - a target of the Enemy…

*Luke 22:31-34*

*31 "Simon, Simon, behold, Satan demanded to have you, that he might sift you like wheat, 32 but I have prayed for you that your faith may not fail. And when you have turned again, strengthen your brothers." 33 Peter said to him, "Lord, I am ready to go with you both to prison and to death." 34 Jesus said, "I tell you, Peter, the rooster will not crow this day, until you deny three times that you know me."*

…still trying to stop it, he again tried to interfere with the will of the Father when they came to get him.

*Luke 22:49-51*

*49 And when those who were around him saw what would follow, they said, "Lord, shall we strike with the sword?" 50 And one of them struck the servant of the high priest and cut off his right ear. 51 But Jesus said, "No more of this!" And he touched his ear and healed him.*

*Matthew 26:50b-54*

*Then they came up and laid hands on Jesus and seized him. 51 And behold, one of those who were with Jesus stretched out his hand and drew his sword and struck the servant of the high priest and cut off his ear. 52 Then Jesus said to him, "Put your sword back into its place. For all who take the sword will perish by the sword. 53 Do you think that I cannot appeal to my Father, and he will at once send me more than twelve legions of angels? 54 But how then should the Scriptures be fulfilled, that it must be so?"*

*John 18:10-11*

*10 Then Simon Peter, having a sword, drew it and struck the high priest's servant and cut off his right ear. (The servant's name was Malchus.) 11 So Jesus said to Peter, "Put your sword into its sheath; shall I not drink the cup that the Father has given me?"*

---

We interfere like Peter interfered. Thank you for your forgiveness, O God! Consider the forgiveness and comfort Jesus gave Peter after his resurrection, after Peter had failed so miserably. Thank you, God, that you bring peace to the mourning and comfort to the sorrowful:

*John 21:15-17, 19b*

*15 When they had finished breakfast, Jesus said to Simon Peter, "Simon, son of John, do you love me more than these?" He said to him, "Yes, Lord; you know that I love you." He said to him, "Feed my lambs." 16 He said to him a second time, "Simon, son of John, do you love me?" He said to him, "Yes, Lord; you know that I love you." He said to him, "Tend my sheep." 17 He said to him the third time, "Simon, son of John, do you love me?" Peter was grieved because he said to him the third time, "Do you love me?" and he said to him, "Lord, you know everything; you know that I love you." Jesus said to him, "Feed my sheep. ...19b ...And after saying this he said to him, "Follow me."*

---

When we work to accomplish *our* will, seeing what we think we know for sure, we must keep in mind that we just might be resisting the workings of God our Father. Don't be drawn in by Satan's deceptions! God's fruit of the Spirit ways lead us to say and do *his* will, bring Peace that surpasses all understanding and a quiet confidence borne of him. Though in this world we will have trouble, be still and know that he is God! (Psalm 46:10)

*John 13:34-35*

*"A new commandment I give to you, that you love one another: just as I have loved you, you also are to love one another. By this all people will know that you are my disciples (talmidim), if you have love for one another."*

*Matthew 11:28-30*

*28 Come to me, all who labor and are heavy laden, and I will give you rest.*
*29 Take my yoke upon you, and learn from me, for I am gentle and lowly in heart, and you will find rest for your souls. 30 For my yoke is easy, and my burden is light."*

*Isaiah 30:15 NIV*

*This is what the Sovereign Lord, the Holy One of Israel, says: "In repentance and rest is your salvation, in quietness and trust is your strength, but you would have none of it.*

*O God, we deeply desire that our love would be agape love, "preferring" to do your will your way. <u>Teach us and train us in agape love that your kingdom come and your will be done in our lives,</u> **<u>that we not enter into temptation,</u>** <u>that you be glorified.</u>*

*May we not accuse, deliver us from those who would Accuse us. May we not cause division, deliver us from those who would Divide us. May we not judge, deliver us from those who would Judge us. May we not condemn, deliver us from those who would Condemn us. Fill us with your Spirit, your Helper, your Comforter, your Encourager, your Wonderful Counselor – that we reflect your glory to those who are too much in this world. O Spirit, give us the words to say and/or words to pray, and actions in accordance with the Father's will.*

*May we hear you and agree with you, see you and follow you. Like Enoch, may we walk with you! You are our greatest need. Clarify our thoughts, that our words and deeds be in accordance with your will for us – one with you, you in us and us in you. Unite your people in more productive service, O God!*

*Jehovah Nissi (I the Lord am your Conqueror, and the Banner under which to Unite): Unite your people to more productive service worldwide! Show us the errors in our theology, doctrine, systems and structures that we not be a hindrance to your truth working in each life each day. Not by our power or by our might, but by your Spirit – give us wisdom, O God!*

***Lead us not into the test**, but if it be your will to do so, prepare us and strengthen us by your Holy Spirit that we may be found in you, Jehovah Tsidkenu (I am your righteousness), expressing your fruit, your character, your attributes - and be credited as righteous that you be glorified. Bind Evil for your sake that we overcome by the power of your Spirit and according to your will. Give us wisdom, O Helper, to learn from our mistakes that our ways become more and more like your ways. May we not be deceived and act according to our ways against your truth and timing and will. **Let us not be tempted** to continue in our ways or return to our former ways. Be our strength that we not be worn down by continued trials, but do your works in us Father that we overcome by the power of your Spirit. Clarify our thoughts, that our words and actions accomplish your will for us, one with you, you in us and us in you. Dwell in us, Father. Do your works that we **not enter into temptation**.*

*1 Peter 4:12-14*
*12 Beloved, do not be surprised at the fiery trial when it comes upon you to test*
*you, as though something strange were happening to you. 13 But rejoice*
*insofar as you share Christ's sufferings, that you may also rejoice and be glad*
*when his glory is revealed. 14 If you are insulted for the name (believing faith*
*in the power of the presence and in the character and attributes) of Christ, you*
*are blessed, because the Spirit of glory and of God rests upon you.*

*Galatians 5:22-23a*
*22 But the fruit of the Spirit is love, joy, peace, patience, kindness, goodness,*
*faithfulness, 23 gentleness, self-control;*

James 1:2-4

2 Count it all joy, my brothers, when you meet trials of various kinds, 3 for you
know that the testing of your faith produces steadfastness. 4 And let
steadfastness have its full effect, that you may be perfect and complete,
lacking in nothing.

Romans 5:2-5

2 Through him we have also obtained access by faith into this grace in which
we stand, and we rejoice in hope of the glory of God. 3 Not only that, but we
rejoice in our sufferings, knowing that suffering produces endurance, 4 and
endurance produces character, and character produces hope, 5 and hope does
not put us to shame, because God's love has been poured into our hearts
through the Holy Spirit who has been given to us.

Luke 6:22-23

22 "Blessed are you when people hate you and when they exclude you and
revile you and spurn your name (the power of his presence, character and
attributes in you) as evil, on account of the Son of Man! 23 Rejoice in that day,
and leap for joy, for behold, your reward is great in heaven;
for so their fathers did to the prophets.

Isaiah 53:3

He was despised and rejected by men, a man of sorrows and acquainted with grief; and as one from whom men hide their faces he was despised, and we esteemed him not.

Romans 8:28-29

28 And we know that for those who love God all things work together for good,
for those who are called according to his purpose. 29 For those whom he
foreknew he also predestined to be conformed to the image of his Son, in order
that he might be the firstborn among many brothers.

O Jesus, you were called a man of sorrows, well acquainted with grief. You looked upon the lives of those around you when you walked the earth and saw depths that we cannot. Like you, may we not look upon those who are failing us with judgment and contempt, but rather with sorrow for their choices and compassion for their plight. Trusting that you use all things for good, may we instead count it all joy because you are active on our behalf, and that if we will *but agree with you for us, you will grow us and conform us into your image, character and attributes. May we agree with you for us all and rejoice, knowing that you are active for all of our benefit. Turn our sorrow to Joy through our trust in you, and bring your Peace and Joy to those around us.*

*You know what they need (leaders of all kinds and types: extremists, pacifists, military, police, missionaries, governments, The United Nations - every leader from the greatest to the least and the good to the bad!). We agree with you for them and ask that their families, friends and associates would receive your courage - that they influence them and encourage them to do your will,* ***overcoming temptation****, protected by the power of your Spirit, prepared by you, strengthened by you,* ***delivered from Evil****. That each would know you, love you, trust you, learn your ways and act in accordance with your will - that none should perish. Since we are all leaders in at least some small way, that includes us!*

*You have heard the cries of your people, O God. We agree with you that your will be done on earth as it is in heaven. We ask you to send more and more laborers that even our Adversaries be restored to you and avoid self-inflicted destruction! You are bringing your kingdom, even through us!*

*While our politicians fight and incite Division among us, the people they were elected to serve suffer due to their inaction on the greater issues of the day. Give us wisdom at the polling places, O God!*

*By the power of your Spirit, may we* ***overcome the temptation*** *to not trust you. When we see the failings in those around us and begin to fear the loss of our safety, security, reputation, freedom, love, hope, faith – may we turn to you and trust you. What others intend for our harm, you will use for good. You are trustworthy, faithful, forgiving and ever loving. You are El Olam (Everlasting God – patient, wise and all loving); Jehovah Sabbaoth (the Lord of Hosts, when his children have failed he will keep all his promises); Abba (Daddy), El Elohim (the Lord our God and Creator); Jehovah Rophe (the Lord heals, who is our Healer); Jehovah Rohi/Jehovah Raah (the Lord is my Shephard); Emmanuel (God with us); the Holy Spirit – our Wonderful Counselor, Helper, Comforter and Encourager. All good things come from you. You know the good plans you have for us, none to do us harm.*

*Forgive us when we do not trust you to be active to use all things for good in our lives and instead give in to the* ***temptation*** *to abuse the good things you have provided - for purposes beyond which you intended: indulgence in sensuality, intoxicants, tobacco, medicinals, food, materialism/shopping, work, influence, solitary time, attainment of knowledge, attainment of wealth and ____________________________________________(add your own here). When we do not trust you with our lives, these become idols that numb our minds from the ill of the world, the very ill that you gave us to encounter, to affect, to impact, to bring recovery to and restoration from. Rather, may we find comfort in in the Wisdom you give us for surviving the depravity of the Ways of the World.* ***Deliver us from Evil****, make our overseers Peace and our taskmasters Righteousness!*

*By the power of your Spirit, may we* ***overcome the temptation*** *to withdraw from others, to not trust you to be active in our lives for them and to use all things for good. May we not fear rejection, and so choose to avoid reaching out to others in Love. May we have no expectation of others to respond in Love in return, that we may Persevere in sharing and showing and Loving unconditionally.*

*2 Peter 1:3-7*

*3 His divine power has granted to us all things that pertain to life and*
*godliness, through the knowledge of him who called us to his own glory and*
*excellence, 4 by which he has granted to us his precious and very great*
*promises, so that through them you may become partakers of the divine nature,*
*having escaped from the corruption that is in the world because of sinful*
*desire. 5 For this very reason, make every effort to supplement your faith with*
*virtue, and virtue with knowledge, 6 and knowledge with self-control, and self-*
*control with steadfastness, and steadfastness with godliness, 7 and godliness*
*with brotherly affection, and brotherly affection with love.*

*Nehemiah 8:10b*

*And do not be grieved, for the joy of the Lord is your strength.*

*John 14:10*

*Do you not believe that I am in the Father and the Father is in me? The words that I say to you I do not speak on my own authority, but the Father who dwells in me does his works.*

*O God, by the power of your Spirit, may we* ***overcome the temptation*** *to correct that which is not ours to correct.* ***Deliver us from*** *the* ***Evil*** *we would do if we were to act according to our own will, leaning on our own understanding - as we see fit in our minds. Dwell in us, Father, move to bring balance in our hearts, souls and minds. Do your works in us,*
*bring us your Joy that we be strengthened!*

*Prepare us, encourage us, strengthen us, you in us and us in you,* ***overcoming temptation****, protected by the power of your Spirit,* ***delivered from Evil*** *– and accomplish your will for us! Jesus only acts in accordance with the Father's will. May it be true of us, O God. Lead us to will and to do by the power of your Holy Spirit, in the power of your Presence in us and in your character and attributes – producing fruit of the Spirit!*

# Chapter Sixteen

## Deliver Us From Evil

How big is your "us"? My tendency is that it includes my family and friends, but Jesus tells us to pray for all of the people on the earth. That by the power of the Holy Spirit all of us be delivered from Evil. For the coming of his kingdom to all of us – that none should perish.

*1 Timothy 2:1, 3, 4*

*1 First of all, then, I urge that supplications, prayers, intercessions, and thanksgivings be made for all people, ... 3 This is good, and it is pleasing in the sight of God our Savior, 4 who desires all people to be saved and to come to the knowledge of the truth.*

*John 3:16*

*"For God so loved the world, that he gave his only Son, that whoever believes in him should not perish but have eternal life.*

*Matthew 11:28-30*

*28 Come to me, all who labor and are heavy laden, and I will give you rest. 29 Take my yoke upon you, and learn from me, for I am gentle and lowly in heart, and you will find rest for your souls. 30 For my yoke is easy, and my burden is light."*

*1 Peter 2:9*

*But you are a chosen race, a royal priesthood, a holy nation, a people for his own possession, that you may proclaim the excellencies of him who called you out of darkness into his marvelous light.*

*Matthew 28:19-20*

*19 Go therefore and make disciples of all nations, baptizing them in (into) the name (the indwelling Presence) of the Father and of the Son and of the Holy Spirit, 20 teaching them to observe all that I have commanded you. And behold, I am with you always, to the end of the age."*

*Ephesians 6:18*
*praying at all times in the Spirit, with all prayer and supplication. To that end, keep alert with all perseverance, making supplication for all the saints.*

---

*Teach us how to engage. Show us when and where to engage. Show us who & what are ours to engage and who & what are not ours to engage. Unite your people to more productive engagement! May we not speak or act according to our own understanding, but be led by and follow your still small voice - given to us for discernment, for wisdom, for timing, for strength, for* ***deliverance from Evil****, for the good that you intend us to do. That which we fear may be ours to engage. Give us wisdom and clarity and accomplish your works!*

*Hebrews 3:7-9*
*7 Therefore, as the Holy Spirit says, "Today, if you hear his voice, 8 do not*
*harden your hearts as in the rebellion, on the day of testing in the wilderness, 9*
*where your fathers put me to the test and saw my works for forty years.*

*Isaiah 30:15 NIV*
*This is what the Sovereign Lord, the Holy One of Israel, says: "In repentance and rest is your salvation, in quietness and trust is your strength, but you would have none of it.*

*John 6:43-45*
*43 Jesus answered them, "Do not grumble among yourselves. 44 No one can*
*come to me unless the Father who sent me draws him. And I will raise him up*
*on the last day. 45 It is written in the Prophets, 'And they will all be taught by*
*God.' Everyone who has heard and learned from the Father comes to me*

*Luke 12:32*
*"Fear not, little flock, for it is your Father's good pleasure to give you the kingdom.*

---

*Father, all of us have irritating people in our lives, those with whom we have little patience, and with whom we find it easy to justify bad behavior in response to theirs. Train us up in the attitudes of Jesus to communicate humbly with fruit of the Spirit, that we might instead share the information they need to hear with Goodness, Gentleness, Patience, Kindness, Perseverance and Self-Control – these flowing from you through us to them – for all of our benefit.*

*May we not* ***enter into*** *the* ***temptation*** *of Judging them, lest we be judged. Work in our hearts, souls and minds that we forgive them, lest we remain unforgiven.* ***Deliver us from*** *the* ***Evil*** *we would do otherwise as we lean on our own understanding, Justifying our own bad behavior with words like, "They started it!", "They did it to me again!", "It's not my fault!", "I'm not going to put up with it!", "I have a right!".*

*Today when we hear your voice, may we not harden our hearts but accomplish your works. Open our minds past our suppositions, our politics, our personal conflicts and misunderstandings, O God, that we see your will for us and follow you in it. May we seek first your kingdom and your righteousness. Draw us closer and closer to you, strengthening us in Love and understanding, that we become more and more like you and one with you. <u>Father, we agree with you and thank you that you continue to move in the hearts, souls and minds of every man, woman and child on the whole earth; that we each have every opportunity to come to know you, Love you, trust you and be taught by you.</u>*

*Give us your Peace, that we reflect your glory. In quietness and trust may we find your strength and respond to those who wrong us with fruitful words from the Spirit. In repentance and rest we live in you, one with you, and are able to walk out our salvation as you, Father, dwell in us and do your works in us, for the benefit of those around us. Slow our pace, O God, that we hear your still small voice. Still our hearts that we remember that <u>you</u> are God! Your will be done in and through us, not ours, we desire to learn your ways!*

*We ask you to stop us in the moment as we turn to respond in Anger, with Sarcasm, with Harsh Words, a Judgmental spirit, Vengeance, or Retaliation. May we no longer Condemn, Coerce, Demand, Blame or Shame in an attempt to Control others. To make happen what we want to have happen, for our purposes. Rather, lead us to encourage, share, explain, train, inform, coach and describe with your Kindness and Gentleness, in your ways, in Unity with your purpose - and give us ears to hear as well!*

*You are for us! <u>Reveal yourself to us! May we Love you! May we know you, the meaning of our lives and fulfill your will for us, overcoming temptation, protected by the power of your Spirit, prepared by you, strengthened by you,</u>* ***<u>delivered from Evil</u>****<u>. You know what we need, draw us closer, teach us your ways, in our thoughts make us one with you - that we agree with you for us.</u>*

*Strengthen families, O God, **deliver us from Evil**! Rally your people around us and us around them, lead us to minister together as one by the power and Gentleness of your Holy Spirit. We trust that you are active for good in all our lives. May we accept you, Love you, and live in the grace, mercy and Love you continually pour out for us.*

*John 14:21*

*21 Whoever has my commandments and keeps them, he it is who loves me. And he who loves me will be loved by my Father, and I will love him and manifest (root and establish) myself to (in) him."*

*John 14:23*

*23 Jesus answered him, "If anyone loves me, he will keep my word, and my Father will love him, and we will come to him and make our home with him.*

*Proverbs 3:11-12*

*11 My son, do not despise the Lord's discipline or be weary of his reproof,*
*12 for the Lord reproves him whom he loves, as a father the son in whom he delights.*

*James 1:17*

*Every good gift and every perfect gift is from above, coming down from the Father of lights, with whom there is no variation or shadow due to change.*

*1 Timothy 2:3-4*

*3 This is good, and it is pleasing in the sight of God our Savior, 4 who desires all people to be saved and to come to the knowledge of the truth.*

*Matthew 18:14*

*So it is not the will of my Father who is in heaven that one of these little ones should perish.*

*2 Peter 3:9*

*The Lord is not slow to fulfill his promise as some count slowness, but is patient toward you, not wishing that any should perish, but that all should reach repentance.*

*Philippians 1:6*

*6 And I am sure of this, that he who began a good work in you will bring it*

*<u>to completion</u> at the day of Jesus Christ.*

*When you had the option of either creating life and the universe or not, you chose to give life. Had you not given us life, we would have never had the chance at eternity with you. You knew that. Without life, Acceptors would not have had the opportunity to Accept and follow into eternity with you. May those who continue to Reject you come to know you, trust you and Love you as you draw them to yourself, active in their hearts, souls and minds. Thank you for our opportunities to participate with you as you continue to offer every person on earth eternity with you.*

*Thank you for your unending Love and activity in our lives. How precious it is to be Loved by you! Make all of us on this earth more aware of your Presence and more attentive to your Spirit. Thank you that you are moving in the hearts, souls and minds of every man, woman and child, that we each have every opportunity to come to know you, love you and trust you – that none should perish. Draw us closer and closer to you, strengthening us in Love and understanding, as we participate with you and become more and more like you. One with you.*

*Have your way in us always and everywhere, orchestrate our days that you be glorified, that none should perish. Alleluia, perfect is your character and flawless are your attributes! Made as your imagers, grow us more and more to express your fruit, your character and your attributes to those around us each day.*

*Look not at what we truly deserve, but remember the sacrifice of your Son, grant us favor for your sake and* ***deliver us from Evil****. For you alone are Adonai: You alone are Jehovah; You alone are El Elyon, Jesus Christ; with our Wonderful Counselor, Helper and Comforter, the Holy Spirit. For yours is the kingdom and the power and the glory, forever and ever. Precious are you; life giver, peace giver, purpose giver, our deliverer! Your kingdom come, your will be done, on the whole earth as it is in heaven. Alleluia!*

*<u>You are administering your Kingdom, O God! You have implemented your solution for the hearts, souls and minds of all humanity! Refine us, Jehovah Maccadeshem, that we Love like you Love! Replace our hearts of stone and give us new hearts fully after yours! Fill us with your Spirit and Unite us to</u>*

*more productive service together, one with you. Rally us, overcoming temptation, protected by the power of your Spirit, prepared by you, strengthened by you,* ***delivered from Evil****, Uniting your people to more and more productive service!*

*For your Joy and good day, may you feel Loved today. Merciful Father, you are doing a new thing - may we perceive it! We ask that you send more and more laborers and Unite your people to more productive service in the bringing of your kingdom to all people worldwide. May we Love you with our whole heart, soul, mind and strength; our neighbor as our self; and one another as you have Loved us that the world may know that we are yours, are becoming more like you and are inviting them to join us.*

*Father, I ask these things through the precious reconciling covering provided by Jesus' sacrifice, by the power of your Holy Spirit, for your merciful righteousness and in Unity with your will.*

*Thank you that it is all over in the blink of an eye. Thank you that your offer to Accept you or Reject you is for such a brief period of earthly time: our lifetime. Soon, Rejectors will be separated away from you and your Accepting Followers forever. Acceptors will all be safe with you eternally. It's all simply a matter of our choice, and actions that reflect that choice.*
*Send laborers to our Adversaries, O God!*

*Thank you that you had us in mind before you ever created the universe. Thank you that you desire that we seek to know you, Love you and enjoy relationship with you. Thank you for your offer to bring us Peace, Joy and eternal life as Accepting members of your family.*

*Thank you for your Patience and Perseverance*
*while you give us time to accept or reject your gift.*

***Deliver us from Evil****, O God!*

# Chapter Seventeen

## Deliver All Of Us From Evil, O God!

How big is your "us"? My tendency is that it includes my family and friends, but Jesus tells us to pray for all the people on the earth. For the coming of his kingdom to all of us - that none should perish. Our "us" is to be the whole world as well as those certain individuals, groups or nations that he, with specificity, brings to mind. If you agree with him for the requests and petitions you will find here along the way, you will have asked God for every person in the world by the time you finish. **Deliver** all of **us from Evil, O God**!

*1 Timothy 2:1-6*

*1 First of all, then, I urge that supplications, prayers, intercessions, and thanksgivings be made for all people, 2 for kings and all who are in high positions, that we may lead a peaceful and quiet life, godly and dignified in every way. 3 This is good, and it is pleasing in the sight of God our Savior, 4 who desires all people to be saved and to come to the knowledge of the truth. 5 For there is one God, and there is one mediator between God and men, the man Christ Jesus, 6 who gave himself as a ransom for all, which is the testimony given at the proper time.*

*2 Corinthians 10:4-5*

*4 For the weapons of our warfare are not of the flesh but have divine power to destroy strongholds. 5 We destroy arguments and every lofty opinion raised against the knowledge of God, and take every thought captive to obey Christ,*

*Lord, we agree with you for all of us. Thank you that you are moving in all our hearts, souls and minds to strengthen us, drawing us closer and closer to you. Help us, that we not pray with Judgement, but with a clean heart, O God. Give us compassion for the plight of others as we read and feel, and touch us that we pray as we ought:*

- Pray for all of the children of the world! Warring for lives, the Enemy wants to interrupt the passing down of *Wisdom* from generation to generation so that Fools may instead pass along ignorance, selfishness, and lack of vision - that the people perish. Caught up in the physical and focused upon getting their worldly wants, without *Wisdom* children will be out of touch with the Spiritual. Short-sighted, they will never even realize that they are entangled in the war for souls happening all around them – and as they grow into adulthood *become* players in the disintegration of families and nations. Agree with Adonai for the *Wisdom* of *all* children, that they pass *Wisdom* down to their children, while never forgetting that we are *all* his children!

- My Family is listed here:

- My Parent's Family is listed here:

- My Spouse's Family is listed here:

- List friends, relatives, organizations and others as led by God here:

- List those you know who seem especially lost right now:

*Lead, O Spirit, may we follow you to the Abundant Life: homeless people, lost people, impoverished people, abused people, angry people, disconnected people, idle people, oppressed people, damaged people, hurting people, deceived people, the "widows and the orphans". That is all of us!*
*Save us, O God!*

For all the nations and leaders of the world, the children they will affect (the future parents, leaders and politicians of our nations) and *their* parents.

- Please change their hearts, O God. *Willing participants in creative collaboration with you*, we desire that *all of us* personally participate according to your will. Give us justice against our Adversaries:

> **1 Samuel 2: 30-31a, 35 - About Eli -** 30 Therefore the Lord, the God of Israel, declares: 'I promised that your house and the house of your father *should* go in and out before me forever,' but now the Lord declares: 'Far be it from me, for those who honor me I will honor, *and those who despise me shall be lightly esteemed.* 31 *Behold, the days are coming when I will cut off your strength and the strength of your father's house*, …35 And I will raise up for myself a faithful priest, *who shall do according to what is in my heart and in my mind. And I will build him a sure house, and he shall go in and out before my anointed forever*.

> **1 Samuel 13:14 – About Saul -** *But now your kingdom shall not continue.* The Lord has sought out *a man after his own heart*, and the Lord has commanded him to be prince over his people, *because you have not kept what the Lord commanded you*."

> **Acts 13:22 – About David** - And when he had removed him, he raised up David to be their king, of whom he testified and said, 'I have found in David the son of Jesse *a man after my heart, who will do all my will*.'

> **Isaiah 1:18** "Come now, let us reason together, says the Lord: though your sins are like scarlet, they shall be as white as snow; though they are red like crimson, they shall become like wool.

> **Luke 18:1-8** 1 And he told them a parable to the effect that they ought always to pray and not lose heart. 2 He said, "In a certain city there was a judge who neither feared God nor respected man. 3 And there was a widow in that city who kept coming to him and saying, 'Give me justice against my adversary.' 4 For a while he refused, but afterward he said to himself, 'Though I neither fear God nor respect man, 5 yet because this widow keeps bothering me, I will give her justice, so that she will not beat me down by her continual coming.'" 6 And the Lord said, "Hear what the unrighteous judge says. 7 And will not God give justice to his elect, who cry to him day and night? Will he delay long over them? 8 I tell you, he will give justice to them speedily. Nevertheless, when the Son of Man comes, will he find faith on earth?"

> Give us justice against our Adversaries, O God! May they repent, turn to you, be healed, follow you all of the days of their lives and accomplish your will for their lives!
   - List Manipulative Leaders, Divisive Politicians, the Corrupt and the Evil who are operating *in their own understanding* and causing trouble in the world here:

*Jehova Repheka, you give all of us time to return to you and avoid self-inflicted destruction. Please intervene in their hearts. Otherwise, remove their influence and replace them with people of your own.*

*Move in the heavenlies that the principalities and powers be rendered ineffective in their efforts to Deceive us, cause Strife among us and influence us toward Self-Focus & Depravity. Bind and loose according to your will and Unite your people to more productive service, O God.*
***Deliver** all of **us from Evil!***

*Give us Peace & humility each day, Jehovah Shalom (the Lord is our Peace - even under great pressure), that we hear, that we agree, that we see, that we follow, that your will be accomplished in us. May we live as you live, Love as you Love and forgive as you forgive - in Peace.*

*El Olam (Everlasting God - patient, wise and all Loving): For authentic Christ Followers in Community, witnesses reflecting your glory, one in you and you in us, United to more productive service - in Love. Send more laborers, O God!*

*Thank you that you have placed your Holy Spirit within us to whisper to us for our benefit. Clarify our thoughts, that our words and actions be in accordance with your will for us. Make each of us houses of prayer in constant communication with you, in intimate relationship with you, one with you, and Unite each of us together as one with you. Unite your people to more productive service, O God, that your kingdom come and will be done on the whole earth as it is in heaven.*

*Thank you that you are ready, willing and able to* ***deliver us from Evil****, Adonai, that we not* ***enter into*** *the* ***temptation*** *to focus upon ourselves, our wants and our Selfish desires! Thank you that you* ***forgive us our sin*** *and lead us to* ***forgive others*** *that we may be one as you are one, you in us and us in you, led by your Holy Spirit to do the good works you have prepared for us in advance. That* ***each day all would receive their daily bread****, that* ***your will be done****. Fill us with your Holy Spirit, replenish our spiritual and physical supply that* ***your kingdom come*** *in all of us, to all of us, for all of us,* ***on*** *the whole* ***earth as it is in heaven****. That none should perish, that we would all come to know and Love you and be thanking you continuously for all that you have given to us!*

*Glorious are you and your ways!* ***Hallowed be your name!*** *Thank you for the power of your Presence in us, that you are manifesting your character and attributes in us! You are* ***our Father in heaven!*** *We are your children, precious to you and under your constant care! May we respond to your promptings and accomplish the sharing of the Love you point out for us to give! Thank you that we are all taught by you to know how to accomplish these things for all people. Thank you for the Joy of participating with you as we are in you and you in us! You are like no other - perfect is your character, your attributes are flawless! You are growing us in humility, to produce in and through us, fruit of the Spirit. You have always been, and will always be, for us! Precious are you; life giver, peace giver, purpose giver, our deliverer! Peace = Confidence in YOU, O God! Teach us to Love like you, train us up in your ways that we live as you live both today and in eternity with you. AMEN!*

# *Chapter Eighteen*

## Final Thoughts On The Prayers Jesus Taught Us

I hope that you have a new appreciation for the depth of the prayer Jesus taught us to pray. I also hope that you will consider using Chapters 8-14 periodically for the greater work of sitting yourself down with the one true Loving God in 2-3 hours of deep reflection - that he would transform you by the renewing of your mind while he also conforms your heart, soul and mind to his. In it, he will cleanse you of the rubbish of your failures, show you how they were just preparation & sanctification in process and encourage you to keep on going, good and faithful servant.

As we go through our day and notice something, *we need to ask him if he would have us do something about it with him*, or instead agree with him that he accomplish his will for it through others. If his will is for *us to do something*, it will be him leading us to do it by the power of the Holy Spirit, in his loving character and attributes, offering *fruit* of the Spirit. If we are *not to do it*, let's state our agreement with his will for it as he does it in another way. Likely through *other willing participants*. What is most important is that *we be in agreement with him* that *his* will be done in *his* way and according to *his* timing. If we will do this, Peace that surpasses all understanding will be ours. *Obedient* in the knowledge of what is ours to engage and what is not ours to engage, his yoke for us will be easy and his burden upon us light.

*Peace = Confidence in YOU, O God!*

****************

A 2007 Barna Group study found that there is very little difference between the lifestyles & behaviors of people who call themselves Christian and those who do not. The evidence from work done by Pew Research and Gallup regarding people in the USA makes it clear that things are getting worse:

- In 2000, 90% believed in God. In 2022 that number was 81%.
- In 2005, 79% were convinced that God exists. In 2017 that number was 64%.
- In 1971, 90% identified as Christian. In 2008: 77%. In 2019: 65%.
- Between 2009-2019, the percentage of Christians who say they attend church regularly dropped 7%.
- Half of all Christians say they attend church once or twice each month.

- Half of all Christians say they only attend church a few times per year or less.
- In 1999, 73% were members of a church. In 2019 that number was 47%.
- In 2009, 17% identified as atheist, agnostic or "nothing in particular". In 2019: 26%.

Given that half of all Christians say they only attend church a few times per year or less, another study tried to determine the percentage of believers who take the Great Commission of making *talmidim* seriously. Their results? 7%.

*Something must be wrong with our approach*. Check the math, our task is not all that daunting. Using the 7% number from above, if *each* year *each* Christ follower will invest themselves in the life of *one person they know* who is not yet a true follower - within 4 years the entire USA will have had the opportunity to secure their eternity.

**Each One Reach One Each Year:**
- In Year 1: the 7% becomes 14%
- In Year 2: the 14% becomes 28%
- In Year 3: the 28% becomes 56%
- During Year 4: the 56% becomes 100%

Considering the world population, Pew Research states that 31% identify as Christian. Of them, perhaps we could say that 5% take the Great Commission of making *talmidim* seriously. Doing the math again, assuming that every one of the 5% make just one true *talmid* each year, the entire world will have had the opportunity to secure their eternity within 6 years!
- Year 1: 5%
- Year 2: 10%
- Year 3: 20%
- Year 4: 40%
- Year 5: 80%
- During Year 6: The 80% becomes 100%

*Clearly, our problem is not in our numbers, but likely in that our approaches do not grow disciples who care – talmidim with hearts after God.*

Much of what our present day pastor/teachers do explains scripture so as to provide us head knowledge for *life application*. This is the *individualistic* Hellenistic approach, not the *talmidic* approach for *becoming just like our rabbi*

*Jesus – collectively*. This may be the biggest reason that the church in the USA has been in decline for so very many decades.

It is an indictment of the ways of our seminaries, bible colleges, pastors, teachers and parenting down through the generations that these numbers have fallen off so drastically. This because our children are not being raised in knowing and understanding the *Love* of God the Father, Son and Holy Spirit. The children are our future, pray for Wisdom in our children!

*What if we were to change our approach so as to better facilitate hearts after God, in the attitudes of Jesus, emphasizing our need to use words and actions in the fruit of the Spirit, loving wholly and loving only?*
*As imagers of God? In the ways of God?*

We tend to give people the facts and the logic and fight to persuade them for saving faith and helpful actions. Then, after baptism, continue our fact-filled logical approach with weekly *self-help* bible teaching and encouragements to serve. As we keep their brains engaged in thinking it all through, a portion walk away feeling something amiss – and their children miss out on the passing down of the *Love* of God.

As well, we admonish people to read their bibles each day, but many are having difficulty with understanding the God-led life through our current approach. Like the story of Philip and the Eunuch, we need to have the scriptures opened up to us in *life on life* opportunities if we will *comprehend how* to live the God-led life with *hearts* after our Father. With eyes that see and ears that hear. Like the two who encountered Jesus on the road to Emmaus, our hearts will burn as the scriptures are opened up to us.

Jesus availed himself for 40 days after his resurrection to open up the scriptures to small groups of his followers, pointing out the hundreds of hidden treasures of prophecy in the Tanakh (the Old Testament), and connecting the dots *for meaning* so that they in turn could do the same for others. And us for still others as well.

*As we learn to live with hearts after the Father and in the attitudes of the Beatitudes (Jesus' attitudes), this posture and humility will prepare us for fruit of the Spirit language and actions in each and every interaction. Will you pass down the Love of God to your children that they may pass it on to their children's children? Will you pass along the Love of God as he places someone in your path?*

What if our politicians were products of families with belief systems fully informed by the Christology of Jesus? Our Father is revealing it to *you*. Who will reverse the trend?

Over two thousand years ago Jesus started conversationally with just twelve. Through him, in him and with him, hundreds of millions, maybe several billion, now know Adonai today. Surely there is someone with whom we might offer to start meeting conversationally each week. Maybe some of us with a few. Others with more than a few. For the children!

*Matthew 13:16-17*

*But blessed are your eyes, for they see, and your ears, for they hear. 17 For truly, I say to you, many prophets and righteous people longed to see what you see, and did not see it, and to hear what you hear, and did not hear it.*

*Each One Reach One Each Year*

***Our Father in heaven, there is nothing better than your Presence** and your ways! I don't want to be king anymore. Train me up that, one with you, more and more my behavior be in accordance with your character and attributes, and consistent with your reputation.*

***Your kingdom come**. Lead my life. **That your will be done** in my life. May it be true for the whole world, your kingdom coming into all our lives and your will being done in all our lives. **Across this whole earth, as it is in heaven.***

***Direct us in doing our part today, that everyone in the world might be fed.** We greatly desire to participate with you and creatively collaborate with you for the solutions to hunger and poverty in this world. Thank you for your care and provision of both physical and spiritual food. May this be an entire day of communion with you, receiving from you and pouring out what you have given us for the support of others and in support of your purpose in this world, according to your will.*

*Everything we have is yours, we are indebted to you for our very lives! All that we have has come from you, blessed by you not so much to have, but to be able to also give, and generously!* ***Forgive us our selfishness*** *as we lavish your blessings upon ourselves rather than flow them through as blessings to others.* ***Forgive us for what we have left undone*** *as we do not do what you have been leading us to do!* ***Forgive us as we cross the line and trespass*** *into the lives of others, pressuring people to do what we want, attempting to Manipulate and Control outcomes - leaning on our own understanding - that our will be done. May we instead learn to offer, share, describe and explain our position without Malice, Coercion, Manipulation or Veiled Threat.* ***Forgive us our sins in the same way that we forgive those who sin against us, those who are indebted to us, and those who cross the line with us.***

*Father, we need your help that we* ***not enter into the temptation*** *to act on our own! Open up the scriptures to us, O God! We require a better and better understanding of the teachings of Jesus, as you do your works in us and lead us by the power of your Holy Spirit! Give us the mind and attitudes of Christ, fill us with your Spirit and conform us to your character. That, with hearts after yours, we reflect your Love and glory in every interaction! Lead us that we not fail you, but having been prepared and strengthened by the power of your Holy Spirit, we accomplish your will for us.*

***Deliver us from the Evil*** *we would do acting on our own,* ***and deliver us from the Evil of the Satan*** *and all those deceived by him into the works of Darkness. May we not accuse, deliver us from those who would Accuse us. May we not cause division, deliver us from those who would Divide us. May we not judge, deliver us from those who would Judge us. May we not condemn, deliver us from those who would Condemn us.*

*Teach us how to engage. Show us when and where to engage. Your yoke is easy and your burden is light. Show us who & what are ours to engage and who & what are not ours to engage. Unite your people to more productive engagement! May we not speak or act according to our own understanding but be led by and follow your still small voice - given to us for discernment, for wisdom, for timing, for strength,* ***for deliverance from Evil,*** *for the* *good that you intend us to do. Fill us with your Spirit, your Helper, your Comforter, your Encourager, your Wonderful Counselor – that we reflect your glory to those who are too much in this world. O Spirit, give us the words to pray and/or words to say, and actions in accordance with the Father's will.*

*Strengthen us that we Persevere to Patiently speak and act in Goodness, Kindness, Gentleness and Self-Control. In Peace that develops Joy and grows greater Love. For you are Adonai: Father, Son and Holy Spirit. One God, forever and ever. We agree with you and desire to participate with you for the Uniting of your people to more productive service, according to your will.*

*Give us justice against our Adversaries, O God! May they repent, turn to you, be healed, and follow you all of the days of their lives. Lord of the harvest, send laborers! Desirous for the accomplishment of your will, we ask all these things here in your precious Presence and in full agreement with your will, that none should perish, and that our Joy may be complete. Amen!*

To receive additional free copies please contact:
One Kingdom Worldwide
One@OneKingdomWorldwide.org

PDF files of this book may be legally shared.

All of the charts and posters in the Life, Love and Leading books are available for free download at OneKingdomWorldwide.org

Revised April 2026

www.ingramcontent.com/pod-product-compliance
Lightning Source LLC
La Vergne TN
LVHW010934110826
845149LV00013B/2592

* 9 7 9 8 9 9 4 5 8 3 9 2 0 *